Child Study and Observation Guide

Gene R. Medinnus

San Jose State University

John Wiley and Sons, Inc.
New York / London / Sydney / Toronto

Library of Congress Cataloging in Publication Data:

Medinnus, Gene Roland
Child study and observation guide.

Includes bibliographical references.
1. Children–Research. I. Title.
BF722.M4 155.4'072 75-15960
ISBN 0-471-59024-X

Printed in the United States of America

10 9 8 7 6 5 4 3 2

Preface

This manual provides the student with a wide range of observational experiences. It is divided into two parts, with fifteen observations in Part I and ten in Part II.

Part I is primarily concerned with the various methods of observation, ranging from longhand recording of a child's behavior in an unstructured situation through more precise methods of recording observational data which focus the observer's attention on specific aspects of behavior. In addition to these general observational techniques, several others that involve more structured ways to obtain information about children are included in Part I. These are questionnaires, interviews, and techniques for appraising personality and ability level. The text provides a discussion of the strengths and weaknesses of each observational method as well as ways in which the method has been used to gather information. In most cases an example is given describing an actual research study that has used the specific technique.

Part II is content oriented in that the observations focus less on methodology and more on important areas of child behavior and development that have received a great deal of attention in current writing and research. The ten observations cover the broad areas of motor development, intellectual ability, language development, and several aspects of social behavior and personality development. An attempt has been made to select highly interesting aspects of behavior that might stimulate the student to further investigation in these areas. The format for these ten observational exercises includes an initial discussion in order to provide the student with a general introduction to the topic. This is followed by instructions regarding the study to be completed. The subjects to be used for the study are listed and the methods for obtaining the data are described. A number of discussion questions are provided to aid the student in drawing conclusions from the data he has collected. Although some of the topics included in this part may seem to involve rather abstract concepts, the explanations provided in the introductions are such that the concepts should be easily understood by a beginning student.

In both Parts I and II the observations involve children ranging in age from infancy through elementary school. Consequently, the student gains firsthand familiarity with the broad sweep of development in many different areas of behavior.

It is recognized that twenty-five observations are more than could be reasonably expected of a student in a single course, whether a quarter or a semester in duration. However, the larger number of observations provides a great deal of flexibility for both the instructor and the student. If the goal of a particular course is to acquaint the student with general methods of child observation, the first four observations, plus Observation 9, "Time Sampling," and several observations from Part II might be required. On the other hand, the instructor may wish to familiarize the student with many different ways of collecting information about children, in which case he might assign Observation 1, "Naturalistic Observation," plus Observations 9 to 15, each of which is concerned with a different technique. The instructor may design the course to emphasize content areas; for this purpose most of the observational exercises in Part II would be required. Since the observations vary in terms of the amount of time required to complete them, the instructor may use this as a basis for selection. In addition, he may scale down the suggested requirements for any given observation. For example, in Observation 15 involving interviews with mothers, it is suggested that four mothers be interviewed. This number may be reduced to one or two. In a one-semester "pilot testing" of the manual I found it useful to assign different observations to different students so they could all profit, through exchanging experiences in class discussions, from the entire range of observations.

A number of references to books and journal articles are included at the end of the discussions of each of the methodological techniques described in Part I and at the end of each of the observations in Part II. These direct the student to further readings to broaden his understanding of the various methodological approaches and the various content areas of child development. Some of the references date back to the 1930s and 1940s, and some even earlier. Most of these refer to classic studies in the history of child development. Students of child observation should be familiar with these studies and with the contributions they have made to our understanding of child behavior. Moreover, these early studies highlight the fact that it was only natural and appropriate that the early writers and researchers in the field of child development were concerned with the ways to collect data about children. This continued concern with the refinement of observational and research techniques culminated in the publication in 1960 of the comprehensive *Handbook of Research Methods in Child Development.*

The purpose of this manual is twofold: to familiarize the student with the various techniques that have been developed to study and observe children; and to provide the student with a firsthand and intimate acquaintance with children and with the many factors that influence their behavior and development. A by-product of the first purpose is that familiarity with some of the methods basic to research with children assists the student in judging the merits of a study in terms of the design and procedures employed. Every methodological technique has its strengths and weaknesses, and these become apparent when they are used. Moreover, through research experience, the student is in a better position to evaluate the conclusions of a research investigation. Are they warranted by the data?

I hope that the student will become so fascinated with the endless facets of child behavior that his curiosity will lead him to a lifelong inquiry into the roots of human behavior, whether in himself or in others.

Gene R. Medinnus

Contents

Introduction

WHY STUDY CHILDREN?

There are many reasons why the study and observation of child behavior has occupied the attention of adults for a very long time.

1. The intellectual curiosity of individuals with a scientific turn of mind prompts them to examine with great interest and intensity a variety of natural phenomena. The history of man's scientific interest in his natural environment dates back many centuries. Certainly, one might argue that people are the most important aspect of that environment. Consequently, much effort has been devoted to the study of human behavior. In the words of Alexander Pope, "The proper study of mankind is man." Literature contains numerous references to children, their behavior, their activities, and their view of the world. Furthermore, children have been the subject of paintings throughout the history of art, perhaps particularly in Western culture. To summarize, children have been considered proper subjects for investigation in man's quest to understand the world within and around him.

2. We must understand children in order to guide their behavior. It has become almost a truism that the more we learn about a given individual, the better the position we are in to understand what "makes him tick"—why he behaves as he does, why he functions as he does, and what purposes his various actions and attitudes serve. Much of human behavior is learned, and thus by observing a child in a variety of "learning settings"—the home, the classroom, the playground, the neighborhood—we can come to understand some of the reasons for his behavior. Through such observations, deviations in behavior and functioning can be identified and appropriate measures can be adopted to assist the child. Child guidance workers,

including school psychologists and clinical child psychologists, are well trained in interpreting and understanding behavior and learning problems and in formulating approaches to solve these problems. While there are exceptions, most theories, and the procedures based on these theories, for remediating various emotional and learning problems involve an initial diagnostic phase followed by remedial procedures. A great many diagnostic techniques have been developed, ranging from observing the child's behavior in a number of situations to rather sophisticated diagnostic tests. For example, in formulating a remedial plan for a third-grade child who is experiencing difficulties in reading, reading diagnostic tests are administered. The precise nature of the child's reading problem is identified and, on this basis, a reading program is developed.

3. Another reason for studying children relates to the strong and continuing concern of behavioral scientists with prediction. This concern among early child developmentalists focused on physical growth. Many studies attempted to predict adult height and weight from repeated measures taken throughout the childhood years. These longitudinal studies, which followed the same individuals over a considerable period of time, found that, barring marked deviations in the environment, physical characteristics are highly stable so that prediction, with a fair degree of accuracy, is possible. Later, with the development of a reliable measure of intelligence, many research investigations dealt with that area of behavior. Again, a fair degree of predictability was discovered but, for a variety of reasons, predictive accuracy was less than that for physical growth. Some of these reasons stemmed from the measuring instruments themselves, while others were related to changes in the nature of intelligence—qualitative changes in intellectual functioning—throughout the developmental years. More recently, attention has been given to the possibility of predicting personality development and emotional adjustment. Can one predict, from personality assessments made in the early years, later personality and emotional adjustment? How much continuity and stability is there over an extended period of time in the personality domain? Are various personality characteristics—sociability, disposition and mood, adaptability—formed

early and only minimally affected by subsequent environmental events? Answers to some of these questions assist the child psychologist in prescribing preventive measures in the mental health area. This point clearly relates to the previous one concerning guiding children's behavior.

4. The fourth reason, related to the first, for the great interest shown in studying children is man's desire to understand himself. Freud added further support to the long-held belief that "the child is father of the man", and in order to understand ourselves, we must understand the child within us. In other words, we must try to understand the role played by our childhood experiences in shaping our adult behavior. In fact, Transactional Analysis, a recently popular approach used in group psychotherapy, is founded on the notion that within each of us there are three figures: an Adult (rational, objective, and decision making), a Parent (incorporated largely from the behavior of our own parents toward us but from other early authority figures as well), and a Child (carefree, joyful, dependent, and demanding). An understanding of which of these three "tapes" are playing in a given situation, or which of these "selves" are doing the talking, gives us insight into our own inner personality dynamics.

A NOTE ON OBSERVATIONAL METHODS

While observation may take a variety of forms, looking at and recording the behavior of the subject under study are the basic elements in all. Although observation may appear to be a very simple procedure, a great deal of training and experience are required in order for the observer to become skilled at making accurate and meaningful observations. Moreover, observation may range, in terms of sophistication, control, and precision, from longhand recording of a child's behavior to the use of complicated recording equipment in which the observational data are fed into a computer for quantification and analysis. The reason for the observation may range from a desire to learn about behavior to a research attempt to test a specific hypothesis drawn from a theory of human behavior.

Part I

Methodology and Examples of Observations

This part is divided into two sections. In Section A the various observational methods and techniques are discussed. One or more observations, to be completed by the student, are presented for each of the methods described. These observational studies are included in Section B.

Section A

Discussion of Methodology

In this section a number of observational approaches will be examined. These are divided into three main categories, with a treatment of specific observational methods under each of the broad areas. Baby biographies and psychological ecology are described under the heading, "Naturalistic Observation." "Controlled Approaches to Observation" includes four techniques: time sampling, event sampling, rating scales, and miniature situations. The following procedures are discussed in the category, "Other Child Study Methods": which includes questionnaires and inventories, personality appraisal techniques and psychometric tests of ability, and interviews. In a general way the sequence of the observational methods surveyed proceeds from observations in which little or no control is exercised over the subject of the observation and in which recording of the behavior observation is unstructured to methods which structure both the subject and the recording of preselected behaviors.

NATURALISTIC OBSERVATION

In naturalistic observation, the behavior of children is recorded without the use of any predetermined categories, check lists, or arbitrary time intervals. An attempt is made to record all of the observable ongoing behavior.

Baby Biographies

Perhaps the oldest form of naturalistic observation was the diary-type accounts of the behavior of an individual child. These early anecdotal accounts, usually written by an interested parent or relative, date back to the 1800s. Frequently no attempt was made to separate the recording of observable behavior from an interpretation of that behavior. Often, too, various motives were imputed to the child and, very likely, these motives were a projection of the observer's own needs, feelings, and biases. Although unsatisfactory in many ways from a scientific point of view, these early baby biographies provided some normative information on the appearance of various developmental behaviors, such as the average age of sitting up, crawling, walking, and talking. Clearly, however, the subjects of the diaries were not randomly selected from the general population; indeed, they were not selected to be representative of any particular group of children. They were available for observation to an adult who typically was well educated and who possessed an unusual curiosity about human behavior.

Darwin's interest in the biological origins of behavior is evident in the following excerpt from an observational account of one of children:

> During the first seven days various reflex actions, namely sneezing, hiccoughing, yawning, stretching, and of course sucking and screaming, were well performed by my infant. On the seventh day, I touched the naked sole of his foot with a bit of paper, and he jerked it away, curling at the same time his toes, like a much older child when tickled. The perfection of these reflex movements shows that the extreme imperfection of the voluntary ones is not due to the state

> of the muscles or of the coordinating centers. At this time, though so early, it seemed clear to me that a warm soft hand applied to his face excited a wish to suck. This must be considered as a reflex or an instinctive action, for it is impossible to believe that experience and association with the touch of his mother's breast could so soon have come into play. During the first fortnight he often started on hearing any sudden sound, and blinked his eyes. The same fact was observed with some of my other infants within the first fortnight. Once, when he was sixty-six days old, I happened to sneeze, and he started violently, frowned, looked frightened, and cried rather badly: For an hour afterwards he was in a state which would be called nervous in an older person, for every slight noise made him start. A few days before this same date, he first started at an object suddenly seen; but for a long time afterwards sounds made him start and wink his eyes much more frequently than did sight; thus when one hundred and fourteen days old, I shook a pasteboard box with comfits in it near his face and he started, whilst the same box when empty or any other object shaken as near or much nearer to his face produced no effect. We may infer from these several facts that the winking of the eyes, which manifestly serves to protect them, had not been acquired through experience. Although so sensitive to sound in a general way, he was not able even when one hundred and twenty-four days old easily to recognize whence a sound proceeded, so as to direct his eyes to the source.
>
> (Darwin, 1877, in Dennis, 1951)

In summary, the baby biographies represent early attempts to observe and record the ongoing complexity of child behavior. While many of the biographies consisted primarily of unstructured observations, others involved some attempt to elicit specific behaviors by administering various kinds of stimulation to the infant. An example of this from the above quote was Darwin's exploration of early reflex behavior. The baby biographies can be considered as pioneer efforts to map the terrain in a well-known but largely unrecorded area. They formed the foundation for the present-day scientific study of human development.

Observations 1-5 on 61 to 79, illustrate various aspects of a naturalistic approach to child observation.

SELECTED BIBLIOGRAPHY

Anderson, J. E. Methods of child development. In L. Carmichael (Ed.), *Manual of child psychology.* New York: Wiley, 1954. See pages 1-2.

Blurton-Jones, N. G. (Ed.), *Ethological studies of child behavior.* London and New York: Cambridge University Press, 1972.

Darwin, C. A biographical sketch of an infant. *Mind,* 1881, **6**, 104-107. Reprinted in W. Dennis (Ed.), *Readings in child psychology.* New York: Prentice-Hall, 1951.

Dennis, W. A biography of baby biographies. *Child Development,* 1936, **7**, 71-73.

McGrew, W. C. *An ethological study of children's behavior.* New York: Academic Press, 1972.

Shinn, M. W. *The biography of a baby.* Boston: Houghton Mifflin, 1900.

Sully, J. *Studies of childhood.* New York: Appleton, 1903.

Wright, H. F. Observational child study. In P. Mussen (Ed.), *Handbook of research methods in child development.* New York: Wiley, 1960. See pages 79-83.

Psychological Ecology

The approach developed by Barker and Wright at the University of Kansas is similar to the baby biographies. It involves the study of behavior in natural settings. A trained observer records in detail the behavior of a child in the course of his everyday activities. These psychologists and their coworkers have established and manned a Midwest Field Station in a small town in Kansas comparable in many respects to a marine biology station in the sense that the main purpose of both is to study the behavior and environment of the phenomena under investigation.

Psychological ecologists argue that information obtained from laboratory research on children may be quite different from that obtained by observing the child in a natural setting because of the contrived and artificial nature of the laboratory situation. Moreover, topics that may be of great theoretical interest and concern to psychologists may not be that significant in the daily lives of children. For example, a well-known study (Barker, Dembo, & Lewin, 1943) frustrated a group of very young children by not permitting them to play with some attractive toys placed within sight but out of reach. The results were dramatic. The children regressed to a much less mature and less constructive form of play. However, when children were observed in their day-to-day activities, relatively few instances of frustration, defined as goal blocking, were recorded. Furthermore, when frustration did occur, responses to it were not severe; only mild reactions were noted.

In the ecological approach a deliberate attempt is made to avoid interfering with the ongoing stream of behavior. Even in the physical sciences it is sometimes difficult for the scientist to avoid altering the phenomenon under investigation. How much more likely this would seem to occur when one is studying human behavior. Barker and Wright argue, however, that children are particularly unselfconscious and that, in general, people cannot for long behave in ways different from their characteristic pattern of behavior. A guest in a home for more than a few days can attest to the change from an initial accommodation to the presence of an observer to a more informal mode later that probably typifies the family's day-to-day interaction. However, a word of caution: an observer must guard carefully against altering or modifying in any way the behavior of the individual or individuals under observation. When it appears likely that some alteration has occurred, the observer must attempt to assess the extent and manner in which the behavior has changed. For example, an unusually self-conscious child may become even more so if he is aware that he is being observed. The observer must remain as inconspicuous and unobtrusive as possible, appearing to focus on a group of children rather than on a single child.

The written account of a child's ongoing behavior is called a *specimen record. One Boy's Day* (Barker & Wright, 1951) is a record of an entire day in the life of seven-year-old Raymond Birch. As with other naturalistic approaches to observation, psychological ecology has problems of quantification of the data. Several categories have been devised in order to organize the data in meaningful ways. *Behavior episodes* are units of behavior that describe a particular situation and some ongoing activity in that setting. The following is an excerpt from a specimen record of the interaction between a mother and her children at lunchtime. The behavior episodes are indicated.

Mother: S to have milk

Rene requests matter-of-factly, "I want a drink of milk."

She looks over at her mother as she says this.

The mother walks a few steps to the refrigerator.

She starts to pull at the refrigerator door but turns abruptly.

She walks the few steps to where Peter is.

She leans over and kisses him affectionately on the back of the neck.

Peter smiles a broad smile as if really enjoying this attention.

The mother immediately turns back to the refrigerator. She reaches for the refrigerator handle as she turns.

Mother: S to have juice

"I want some juice," says Rene more firmly as if she has changed her mind.

"No, there isn't any juice made," says the mother as if she is considering this, "How about milk?"

"No", Rene insists firmly.

"We can *make* some," Rene explains as if she insists that her suggestion be followed.

"How about chocolate milk?" asks the mother as if Rene will surely say, "yes," to this.

"You can *make* some," says Rene much more insistently, her voice rising in pitch. "You can *make* some," she repeats insistently.

"You can *make* some juice," she repeats again loudly, her face frowning.

"Orange juice?" queries the mother as if trying to make sure she understands what Rene wants.

"Mmmm hmmm," asserts Rene agreeably.

"We *can* make some orange juice," agrees the mother as she reaches for the freezer part as if to get out some orange juice.

Rene shouts, "*No*! *Kool-Aide*!" as if the mother should have understood this in the first place.

The mother closes the refrigerator door.

Mother: S to know she may have Kool-Aide

She walks over toward the stove area.

She takes a few steps to another cupboard from which she gets the Kool-Aide.

As she does this, she hums a part of the tune that is on the record player and takes several dancing steps.

(Schoggen, pp. 20.03-5 – 20.03-6)

Another category, *behavior setting,* has been defined as "a stable part of the physical and social milieu of a community together with an attached standing pattern of human behavior" (Wright, 1956). Citizens of all ages of Midwest spent the designated number of person hours in the following behavior settings in one year:

18,525 in Clifford's Drug Store,
7,600 in the Second Grade Classroom,
7,300 in Hooker's Tavern,
3,750 in the Methodist Regular Worship Service,
1,000 in the City Library, and
344 in the Brownie's Regular Meeting

(Wright, 1956, p. 266)

The importance of behavior settings, according to the psychological ecologists, is that they dictate to a marked degree the behavior of individuals in that setting. The expected patterns of behavior in Hooker's Tavern are clearly different from those in the Methodist Regular Worship Service.

Several advantages and disadvantages of the ecological approach to observing and understanding child behavior should be mentioned. The approach does capture the full range, richness, and complexity of behavior. Check lists, observation schedules, and other such devices are not employed; consequently, according to advocates of this method, nothing intervenes between the observer and the subject of the observation. The child is studied in naturally-occurring situations in his life. Using the behavior episodes and the behavior settings, one can examine a great number of psychosociological variables: age differences in the number of different behavior settings frequented and the amount of time spent in the various settings; the effects of community size and density on the life patterns of children and adults; differences among children in the duration of their behavior episodes; and the range of activities engaged in by people of various ages.

Despite attempts at quantification by the ecologists, this remains a problem. Identifying the relations among variables is difficult. Furthermore, since children are seen in varying situations, one cannot readily compare their behavior, such as is possible when they are exposed to a standard situation as in intelligence tests, a specific learning task, or a carefully arranged social situation.

In summary, the ecological approach has alerted us to the importance of observing children in their natural habitat: the home, the school, the playground, and the streetcorner. It is a somewhat cumbersome and time-consuming method, however, and the data obtained are not easy to interpret or analyze.

A Recent Refinement of Psychological Ecology

Impressed with the importance of viewing the child in relation to his environment, Caldwell and associates have developed a behavioral coding system for analyzing interactions between individuals and between an individual and his environment. Behavior is likened to a grammatical clause in which there are four basic components: the subject (who or what does something); the predicate or action of the clause (what is done); the object of the clause (toward whom or what the action is directed); and the qualifiers (adverbs) which provide supplementary information. Each of the many categories under the four components is assigned a numerical code that permits the coding of the ongoing action which in turn can be keypunched for computer analysis.

The behavior record is obtained by an observer stationed near the person or persons being observed; the observer whispers into a small portable tape recorder. This descriptive verbal record is transcribed and the coding is done from the typescripts. Most of the behavior samples are either 20 or 30 minutes in duration. The following is a discussion of a behavior record for a nine-month-old child in attendance at a day

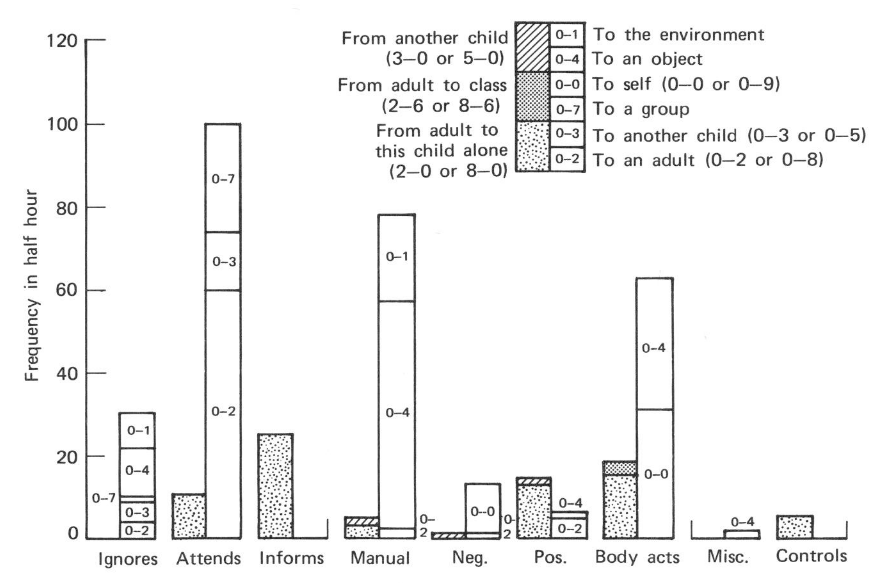

FIGURE 1. Behaviors emitted by a 9-month-old girl and received from adults in a day care center — one half-hour observation.

care center operated by Caldwell and colleagues at Syracuse University. The behavior profile itself is provided in Figure 1.

> The behavior profile of Juanita, a nine-month-old girl, reflects clearly the restriction in range of behaviors possible for a nonmotile, nonverbal infant. Her modal response was "attending", with an adult receiving most of the attention and the remainder divided between another child and a group of children. But more than thirty times the little girl did not respond to (ignored) stimuli considered by the observer to be salient enough to elicit a response. The other major categories of infant behavior were manual activities (manipulating objects, transferring objects to and from the environment) and body activities (non-locomotory and locomotory actions). There were a few episodes of negative emotional response, the majority of which can be recognized as representing whimpers or other signs of distress directed toward no one in particular (identified on the graph as emitted to the self). Likewise there were a few smiles, most of which were directed at one of the adults in the environment. The baby did little else.
>
> (Caldwell, 1969, pp. 93 & 95)

It is apparent that Caldwell's approach to observation possesses advantages over straight observation as well as over the psychological ecology method. First, while the richness and complexity of behavior in natural situations is not lost, ongoing behavior is coded and quantified through the use of meaningful behavioral categories. This permits the observer to identify the specific behaviors that characterize a given child or a given adult. Furthermore, age differences in typical behaviors can be identified, as well as differences among children at a single age level. This method also enables an observer to describe with some precision the characteristics of a child's social and physical environment.. Thus the data can help answer the perennial question posed by behavior scientists: To what extent is an individual's behavior a function of or is influenced by his environment? Are children reared in urban areas different from rural children as a function of their quite different environments? How do differences in the environmental settings contribute to differences in behavior, attitudes, and personality between the adult bushman of the arid Kalihari and the Eskimo of the frozen Lapland?

Observations 6, 7, and 8 on pages 81 to 87 serve to provide the student with experience in the psychological ecology approach to child observation.

SELECTED BIBLIOGRAPHY

Barker, R. G. (Ed.), *The stream of behavior.* New York: Appleton-Century-Crofts, 1963.

Barker, R. G., & Wright, H. F. *One boy's day.* New York: Harper, 1951.

Barker, R. G., & Wright, H. F. *Midwest and its children.* Evanston, Ill.: Row, Peterson, 1954.

Caldwell, B. M. A new approach to behavioral ecology. In J. P. Hill (Ed.), *Minnesota symposia on child psychology. Vol. 2.* Minneapolis: University of Minnesota Press, 1969. Pp. 74–109.

Honig, A. S., Caldwell, B. M., Tannenbaum, J. Patterns of information processing used by and with young children in a nursery school setting. *Child Development,* 1970, **41**, 1045–1065.

Schoggen, M. *An ecological approach to the study of mother child interaction.* Nashville: George Peabody College for Teachers.
Willems, E. P. An ecological orientation in psychology. *Merrill-Palmer Quarterly,* 1965, **11**, 317-343.
Wright, H. F. Psychological development in Midwest. *Child Development,* 1956, **27**, 265-286.
Wright, H. F. Observational child study. In P. Mussen (Ed.), *Handbook of research methods in child development.* New York: Wiley, 1960. Pp. 71-139.

CONTROLLED APPROACHES TO OBSERVATION

While the early baby biographies and the more recent psychological ecology have contributed greatly to our understanding of child behavior, the concern for quantification of the data, as well as other considerations, has prompted researchers to develop a variety of methods for obtaining information from the child and about him. It is true, as the ecologists argue, that the further one is removed from observing the child in his interaction with his environment, the greater is the likelihood of losing some of the richness and complexity of the child's world and the greater the danger of missing some of the important aspects of this world. Moreover, when behavior is taken out of context and reduced to numbers, distortion may result. At the same time, however, it is frequently desirable to be able to quantify the data in order to identify meaningful relations among various child characteristics and in order to make comparisons between groups of children. For example, one might ask: Do boys quarrel more frequently than girls? Do older children quarrel less frequently than younger ones? Is there a relation between frequency of quarreling and IQ, school achievement, physical size, motor ability? Answers to these and other questions can be given when quantifiable data are analyzed.

Time Sampling

One of the earliest methods for quantifying observational data was developed by Willard Olson at the University of Minne-

.. In his study of nervous habits in children, he identified main categories: oral (sucking thumb, biting nails), nasal cking nose, scratching nose), hirsutal (pulling or twisting ir), ocular (rubbing eyes, blinking eyelids), aural (pulling ear, cking ear), and genital (manipulating genitals). The unit of measure was one such behavior per child in a five-minute period. Thus, using 20 five-minute observations, the possible frequency range of each nervous habit per child was 0 – 20. To obtain the data, the observer stationed himself in clear view of the children in the classroom. An ordinary watch with a minute hand was used for recording time.

The following findings emerged from Olson's early study:

> 1. There is no relationship between the amount of nervous habits and age.
> 2. The incidence of nervous habits is significantly greater in girls than in boys.
> 3. Members of a family will resemble each other more closely with respect to nervous habits than will persons selected at random.
> 4. Evidence is presented which suggests that association with persons of nervous habits will produce nervous habits.
> 5. Fatigue during the school day tends to aggravate the manifestations of nervous habits.
> 6. In general, the underweight child will have more nervous habits than the normal at all ages.
>
> (Olson, 1929, pp. 89-90)

Many research investigations through the years have employed the time sampling technique. Behaviors such as quarreling, conflict, cooperation, ascendance, aggression, and mother-infant interaction have been studied. In most studies, the time interval has been shortened from five minutes to under a minute. The appropriate time interval depends on the frequency of occurrence of the particular behavior. For example, a longer time interval would be required for studying curiosity than for studying quarreling since the former appears less frequently. In fact, time sampling may be inappropriate for studying behaviors that, though of great significance, occur irregularly and with low frequency. Examples of such behavior are sympathy, response to success and failure, and frustration. Moreover, time sampling could not be used to study behavior that is not overt (e.g., fantasy behavior) as well as privately occurring behavior (e.g., fire setting).

While a number of modifications of time sampling have been introduced, the technique remains a useful one for determining the frequency of occurrence of various behaviors; in turn, these frequency data can be related to various other measures. Furthermore, the reliability of the behavior can be established by making observations over a period of time. To return to our example of quarreling, repeated observation will reveal the extent to which quarreling is a consistent behavior in children as compared with a randomly fluctuating one or one that is situational in nature. Also, the reliability of the observation can be determined by correlating the simultaneous observations of two observers. Individual observer biasses can be identified, examined, and eliminated, which is a clear advantage over some of the earlier observational approaches. However, several disadvantages of time sampling should be mentioned. First, since usually only one behavior is under study at one time, it is difficult to identify the interrelations among a number of behaviors. Second, the pattern or sequence of ongoing behavior interactions is not recorded by the time sampling methods. Students of human behavior are recognizing the reciprocal nature of human interaction. Humans not only *act* but they *react*. For example, the child affects the parent just as the parent affects the child. This is equally true in child-child interaction in which a child is always responding to the behavior of another child. Behavior never occurs in a vacuum. Third, the data yielded by time sampling seldom reveal cause-and-effect relationships. Time sampling can tell us which children quarrel more than others but it cannot tell us why.

To conclude our discussion of time sampling, the following investigation of visual behavior in infants is a recent example of a studying employing the time sampling technique.

PURPOSE: To examine the relation between the amount of time infants spend at various states at 1 and 3 months of age, and their fixation time to visual stimuli presented at 3¼ months of age.

METHOD:

Subjects: The sample consisted of 42 primiparous mothers and their infants, half boys and half girls.

Procedure: Three naturalistic observations were conducted in the home when the infants were 1 and 3 months of age. Each observation was 6 hours in duration. A modified time sample technique was used for coding the observational data. One minute time samples were used, with checks made on a recording form opposite one of the following appropriate infant states:

1. *Awake.* Infant's eyes were three-quarters or more open for a period of at least 5 seconds and he was neither crying nor fussing.
2. *Drowsy.* Infant's eyes were intermittently opened and closed and/or the infant's eyes were less than three-quarters open and he was neither crying nor fussing. This behavior must have been sustained for a period of at least 5 seconds.
3. *Fusses.* Intermittent protest responses were occurring. Protest sounds were of a low level and/or shallow quality and might be interrupted and blended with vocalizations.
4. *Cries.* Infant made intense, unequivocal, bleating vocalizations that were often shrill, strident, or paroxysmal in quality.

At an average of 3¼ months of age the infants were brought into the laboratory where assessments were made of the amount of time they spent looking at various two-dimensional stimuli. Two series of stimuli were used, one involving geometrical figures and the other consisted of three variations of the human face (social stimuli). Total fixation time (TFT) was the measure used in the analysis.

RESULTS: There was an increase in time *awake* from 1 to 3 months, while the scores on *drowsy* and *cries* showed a decrease. Frequency of *fusses* remained the same.

For males there was a significant correlation (.59) between awake state at 1 month and TFT for social stimuli, and a negative correlation (−.57) between the amount of time they cried during the 3 month observation and TFT for geometric stimuli. For females none of the relationships between states and TFT was significant.

DISCUSSION: For males there appears to be a general characteristic of the organism involving visual behavior since those males who spent the greater amount of time at activity levels that were optimal for visually observing the environment also looked longer at the experimentally presented visual stimuli. However, one might hypothesize that for females, social learning (e.g., interaction with mother) plays an important role in visual behavior.

(Moss and Robson, 1970)

While other methods, such as ratings, might have been used to describe infant state in the above study, time sampling yielded actual numerical scores on the amount of time each infant was observed as either awake, drowsy, fussing, or crying during the six hour total observation time. In turn, it was possible to relate these scores to the infants' visual behavior in the laboratory at 3¼ months of age.

Observation 9, on pages 89 to 91, dealing with dependency behavior provides the student with experience in the use of time sampling.

SELECTED BIBLIOGRAPHY

Arrington, R. Time-sampling in studies of social behavior: A critical review of techniques and results with research suggestions. *Psychological Bulletin,* 1943, **40**, 81-124.

McDowell, E. E. Comparison of time-sampling and continuous recording techniques for observing developmental changes in caretaker and infant behaviors. *Journal of Genetic Psychology,* 1973, **123**, 99-105.

Moss, H. A., & Robson, K. S. The relation between the amount of time infants spend at various states and the development of visual behavior. *Child Development,* 1970, **41**, 509-517.

Olson, W. C. *The measurement of nervous habits in normal children.* Minneapolis: University of Minnesota Press, 1929.

Wright, H. F. Observational child study. In P. Mussen (Ed.), *Handbook of research methods in child development.* New York: Wiley, 1960. See pages 92-104.

Beller, E. K. Dependence and independence in young children. *Journal of Genetic Psychology,* 1955, **87**, 25-35.

Event Sampling

Rather than merely checking the occurrence of a specific behavior, event sampling attempts to describe in detail a behavioral sequence. While coding may occur on the spot or later, the concern is with describing and understanding a particular unit of behavior. The following are some of the behaviors that have been studied using the method of event sampling:

anger outbursts, fear reactions, quarrels, eating behavior, and sympathetic behavior.

As an observational method, event sampling could be said to lie somewhere between psychological ecology and time sampling. An investigation using event sampling would have as its focus a specific class of behavior, such as one of those just mentioned, rather than attempting to describe entire sequences of behavior as in psychological ecological. Turning back to the example of the mother's interaction with her children at lunchtime, although a somewhat broad unit of behavior, event sampling would focus only on lunchtime behavior, and either observe a number of aspects of this in the same family over a period of time or it might observe this unit of behavior in a number of different families. Event sampling can be used both with frequently occurring events as well as with those that occur relatively seldom. While both time sampling and event sampling have as their goal the understanding of a specific type of behavior, they differ in several respects. The unit of measure in time sampling is the occurrence of a given behavior in a certain period of time while in event sampling the unit of measure is the behavior itself, although the frequency of occurrence can be determined in event sampling. As with the ecological approach, the data obtained from event sampling are not as amenable to quantification as those yielded by time sampling although, depending upon the behavior, it is possible to develop various categories for coding a behavior sequence.

Barker (1960) has listed some of the following behavioral events as possible targets for event sampling:

> quarrels, anger episodes, fear episodes, frustration episodes, success episodes, failure episodes, competition episodes, cooperation episodes, problem-solving episodes, actions for others, actions against others, play with pets, play with dolls, solitary play episodes, discipline episodes, illnesses, school recitations, public performances, chores, birth, nursing episodes, weaning episodes, car trips, humor episodes, toilet-training episodes, religious-ritual episodes, new-situation episodes (such as first baths, first school days, introductions to strangers), buying things, being the baby sat with, getting-up episodes, and going-to-bed episodes.
>
> (p. 108)

From an examination of some of these classes of behavior, it becomes clear that there is only a small step between observing naturally- or spontaneously-occurring behavior and "staging" or standardizing the situation in order to more readily make comparisons among children. For purposes of study, one probably would not want to stage quarreling, fear, or anger episodes, but standardized situations have been arranged for observing doll play, cooperation, competition, and problem-solving behaviors.

The following is an abstract of a study employing event sampling in addition to several other measures.

PURPOSE:

The study was designed to answer the following questions:

(a) What are the social interactions that are associated with discipline?
(b) What is the relation between general external conditions and the frequency of discipline?
(c) What disciplinary techniques are employed by parents and what are their effects on the child?
(d) How do various parent and child characteristics affect the discipline used?

METHOD:

Subjects: The sample consisted of 120 mothers of children, 60 boys and 60 girls equally divided among the age levels, 3, 6, and 9 years.

Procedure: The mothers were asked to complete two forms dealing with the discipline they employed with their child over a 3 week period. The Daily Information Sheet: Discipline was designed to get at various events (e.g., sleep, illness) which might have an effect on the occurrence of discipline. The Observational Record: Discipline required the mother to describe the disciplinary situation and to record the following information: time and place of occurrence, duration of incident, the difficulty that arose, methods of control used, persons using the control, issue involved, outcome of the incident, how the child reacted to the use of the disciplinary measures, and how long this behavior lasted. An alphabetical list of 26 methods of control was given to the mother to reduce the amount of writing required.

The mothers and the children's nursery school teachers filled out an adjustment inventory on the children.

RESULTS:

The following major findings emerged from the study:

(1) The primary factor associated with discipline was the age of the child, with a decrease in frequency of discipline with age, and a shift in type of discipline employed.

(2) Reasoning and scolding were the most frequently used types of discipline at all ages. Coaxing and threatening were also fairly high for all age groups. Spanking ranked fourth for the three year olds, seventh for the six year olds, and disappeared from the first ten for the nine year olds. Taking away privileges increased in usage from three to nine. Removing the child forcibly appeared in the top ten for the three year olds only, while appeal to the self-esteem of the child appeared only at the nine year level.

(3) Discipline arose in situations where the child was involved in routines of daily living, establishing sibling and adult relationships, and in displaying behavior that adults deemed inappropriate.

(4) Mothers were the persons most frequently responsible for discipline. There was a degree of similarity between mothers and fathers in control methods used.

(5) Duration of disciplinary episodes was relatively brief.

(6) As the day progressed there was greater likelihood for discipline to occur.

(7) The younger child tended to be more variable in his reactions to discipline than the older child.

DISCUSSION:

The increase with age in communication skills leads to smoother parent-child relationships with a consequent decrease in disciplinary episodes. While most children yield in the disciplinary situation, the longterm effects of various types of control methods remain to be identified.

(Clifford, 1959)

Observation 10, on pages 93 to 94 requires the student to choose and observe a frequently occurring behavior in order to gain firsthand experience in the use of the method of event sampling.

SELECTED BIBLIOGRAPHY

Clifford, E. Discipline in the home: A controlled observational study of parental practices. *Journal of Genetic Psychology,* 1959, **95**, 45-82.

Dawe, H. C. An analysis of two hundred quarrels of preschool children. *Child Development,* 1934, **5**, 139-157.

Goodenough, F. L. *Anger in young children.* Minneapolis: University of Minnesota Press, 1931.

Wright, H. F. Observational child study. In P. Mussen (Ed.), *Handbook of research methods in child development.* New York: Wiley, 1960. See pages 104-108.

Rating Scales

A great many rating scales and check lists have been devised for quantifying impressions gained from observation. Clearly, ratings do not take the place of observation; rather, they are a means of summarizing such observations. An assumption underlying some rating scales is that personality is composed of a variety of fairly discrete traits, and that by assessing these, it is possible to write a personality description of an individual child and thus to understand and explain his behavior. Other rating scales are very broad in nature and represent such global characteristics as general adjustment.

Since rating scales are attempts to quantify observation, the validity of such ratings depends largely on the adequacy of the observations that the ratings are based. The adequacy is determined by the amount of time spent observing the child as well as by the number of different settings and situations in which he is observed. To some extent, the more specific the behavior or the trait to be rated, the more selective one can be in his observations and, consequently, the less time is required for an adequate observational sampling of behavior. For example, it would be sufficient to observe a relatively few samples of the child's interaction with peers in order to rate him on a dominative-submissive dimension. On the other hand, many observations would be required to rate a child on "general adjustment to the classroom situation."

Perhaps the recent trend away from ratings, rankings, and check lists is justifiable. Although a numerical rating on a variety of dimensions may help us to understand a child's level of functioning compared with other children, such a "score" tells us little about the causes of behavior and little concerning the most appropriate approach to be used in dealing with the child. A more serious criticism of rating scales is that the rater is seldom required to specify the precise behaviors on which the ratings were based. Different observers perceive and interpret behaviors quite differently and weigh them in different proportions; each of us operates from our own unique frame of reference. While it is relatively easy to establish inter-rater agreement on a rating scale by correlating the ratings made by two observers, one cannot always be sure that another rater, using the scale at a later time, will share the earlier observers' bases for rating a particular dimension. However, establishing a high inter-rater agreement or inter-rater reliability does tend to eliminate individual biasses and distortions.

With regard to the extent of agreement between ratings and other measures of the same characteristic, it is possible to determine such agreement if the behavior is described with a fair amount of precision. When, for example, high agreement is found between ratings of aggressiveness and observational recording of frequency of aggressive behavior, then confidence in the validity of the rating is established. However, when the agreement between two such measures is low, either the ratings are biassed or distorted or the two measures are actually concerned with different behaviors. An interesting example of a marked discrepancy between teacher ratings and other measures was uncovered in a study of the relation between activity level, motor inhibition, impulsivity and IQ in children (Loo & Wenar, 1971). No relation was found between the teacher's rating of activity level and an actual measure of activity level determined by placing an actometer on the child's dominant wrist and ankle for 1½ to 2 hours. In addition, no relation was found between ratings of the child's ability to inhibit motor movements and the child's ability to do so in two laboratory tests designed to assess this characteristic. Clearly teacher biasses explained part of these discrepancies since teachers rated boys as more active than girls and as having less inhibiting control than girls even though the objective measures of activity level and motor inhibition showed no sex difference.

Ratings have been used primarily to assess various personality dimensions although some ratings scales have been devised for physical and intellectual characteristics. Despite some of the criticisms and limitations of ratings mentioned above, they do yield quantitative scores that can be used to study such important topics as the stability and change in a number of child characteristics over time and the relation among such characteristics and other factors (e.g., parent variables).

The following is an example of a study using a rating scale for assessing children's adjustment to the first grade situation:

PURPOSE:

To study the relation between several parental attitude and behavior factors and the child's early adjustment to school.

METHOD:

Subjects: Two groups of first grade children were identified: 10 well adjusted children and 9 poorly adjusted children. Information was also obtained from the 19 sets of parents.

Procedure: Several instruments were employed to assess parent attitudes and parent behavior during the year prior to the child's school entrance. Each of the parents completed a parent attitude questionnaire dealing with a number of aspects of family life, childrearing, and family relationships. In addition, based on interviews with the mothers, the homes were rated on 15 of Fels Parent Behavior Rating Scales which defined 3 major factors: (a) Dependence vs. Independence Encouraging, (b) Democratic vs. Authoritarian, and (c) Degree of Organization in the Home.

Near the end of the children's first grade year, their teacher rated them on a 52-item First Grade Adjustment Scale tapping 5 areas: Physical Status, Social Behavior, Emotional Behavior, Intellectual Abilities, and Adjustment to Classroom Requirements. Each item was placed on a 5-point scale ranging from poor to good adjustment in that aspect of behavior.

RESULTS:

1. Few significant differences were found between the two groups of parents on the attitude scale.

2. The homes of the well-adjusted children were rated higher than the homes of the poorly-adjusted children on the following scales; General Babying, Child Centeredness of Home, General Protectiveness, Justification of Policy, and Accelerational Attempt.

DISCUSSION:

While the negative findings for the attitude measure might suggest that parent attitudes are not important in affecting the child's early school adjustment, the significant results obtained for the maternal behavior ratings discount this interpretation. These latter ratings seem to indicate a difference between the mothers of the two groups of children with regard to acceptance of the child, with the mothers of the poorly adjusted children demonstrating nonnurturant, nonsupportive behavior growing out of rejection. This maternal rejection interferes with the child's normal functioning in the school situation. While the present research did not obtain a measure of the children's self acceptance, it seems likely that children who are not accepted by their mothers will be low in self acceptance. In turn, this leads to poor acceptance by peers which is related to maladjustment.

(Medinnus, 1961)

Observation 11, on pages 95 to 99, involves observing and rating infant behavior.

SELECTED BIBLIOGRAPHY

Cobb, K., Grimm, E., Dawson, B., & Amsterdam, B. Reliability of global observations of newborn infants. *Journal of Genetic Psychology,* 1967, **110**, 253-267.

Loo, C., & Wenar, C. Activity level and motor inhibition: Their relationship to intelligence-test performance in normal children. *Child Development,* 1971, **42**, 967-971.

Medinnus, G. R. The relation between several parent measures and the child's early adjustment to school. *Journal of Educational Psychology,* 1961, **52**, 153-156.

Wright, H. F. Observational child study. In P. Mussen (Ed.), *Handbook of research methods in child development.* New York: Wiley, 1960. See pages 113-114.

Miniature Situations

In discussing event sampling the point was made that there is a small step between observing naturally-occurring segments of behavior as in event sampling and attempting to standardize the situation by introducing various controls in order to elicit specific kinds of behavior. Miniature situations represent an attempt to improve on the ecological approach to collecting data by controlling, standardizing and delimiting the setting as well as the kinds of behavior that are expected to occur. At the same time, the subject is permitted to behave in a natural manner. The assumption underlying this method is, of course, that the child's behavior in the controlled situation is representative of his behavior in similar situations in his daily life. Thus, one might argue that the more closely the miniature situation approximates a real-life situation, the more confidence the investigator may have in his research results.

The miniature situations method has been used primarily to examine various personality dimensions. In fact, some of the research has been clinical in nature in the sense that it has explored individual cases, particularly children and families with emotional problems. There is a distinction between research whose aim is to understand the dynamics operating in a single case versus that which sets out to examine theoretical questions or to establish relationships among variables (e.g., children from autocratic homes tend to be less curious and less creative than those from democratic homes). However, both approaches contribute to our understanding of some of the general principles governing human behavior.

In their research, psychologists have sought to develop shorthand methods of gaining information about the child's behavior, personality, and functioning. As we shall continue to emphasize, there is no substitute for direct observation of the child's day-to-day behavior; yet, there is a demand, both in clinical work with children and in research, for means of assessment that are economical in terms of amount of information gained in a short period of time. For this reason, questionnaires, psychometric instruments, and miniature situations have been developed.

Probably Hartshorne and May's (1928) study of honesty in children was one of the first to use miniature situations. In their study, children were exposed to a variety of real-life situations that afforded them the opportunity to exhibit honest or dishonest behavior. One of the measures of deception involved four athletic tests: the dynamometer test, the spirometer test, pull-ups, and standing broad jump. The children were led to believe that the tests were part of a real athletic contest in which badges were to be awarded to the winners of the four events. The directions for each test were given to the children individually and they were asked to try each procedure, the examiner taking mental note of their performance. Subsequently, the child was told to proceed alone, recording the best of several trials. The difference between the examiner's rating and the child's own was the measure of deception. Selected general findings of the study indicated older children to be slightly more deceptive than younger ones. Few sex differences were noted. The more intelligent children cheated less. Children who showed symptoms of emotional instability were more likely to be deceitful than others.

Another early study that observed children's reactions in controlled situations was the Jersild and Holmes (1935) investigation of children's fears. Children who manifested specific kinds of fears were exposed repeatedly to situations arousing such fears, and their reactions were observed. For example, a group of children who were afraid to enter a dark room were exposed individually to a situation in which the child and the experimenter played with a ball. It was arranged that the ball would go into an adjacent darkened room, and the child was asked to retrieve it.

Later, children's play has been observed in controlled situations where certain types of materials have been provided in order to elicit specific types of responses. Materials such as clay, play dough, cold cream, and finger paints have been used. The rationale for this approach is that the natural language of children is play and that in a permissive, unstructured situation, children will reveal and express their inner needs, hostilities, anxieties, and tensions. The following is an example of some of the behaviors and behavior dynamics that can be observed in such play settings; in this particular setting the children were encouraged to play with dough.

Another little girl whispered "I can't" at first, and approached the dough almost tentatively. She ran her hand in a gingerly way through the mess, and did not squeeze the dough until the experimenter had done so. However, when she did, she squeezed *very* hard, with a kind of aggressive violence which no other child showed. After more play she volunteered, however, "I don't think it's nice." Yet when the experimenter started to put away the pan, she resisted: "I'm not all finished yet." She shook her hands through the mess saying, "Gooey, gooey, gooey!" She squeezed, made balls of the dough. But at the end, after she had washed her hands, she said, "I never want to do that again ... why did you do this to me?" Her expressive face appeared "mildly horrified and puzzled," wanting rapport at the beginning; after being released by the experimenter's example she was definitely aggressive with the paste, in contrast to the other children, and then seemed to develop a sense of guilt as she went on, apparently feeling this was naughty. Among other comments made in the context of cleaning up after the dough, she said, "My mother spanks me if I'm naughty ... I cry so the neighbors hear ... sometimes I scratch her and she spanks me."

(Murphy, 1956, p. 124)

The use of dolls representing family members is a somewhat more organized attempt to elicit information concerning a specific area: the child's perception of the interrelationships within his family. Many investigations along this line have been conducted, with the preschool child the object of study in most cases. Various categories have been used to record the children's behavior, including the following: aggressiveness, with object of aggression noted; affection; sexual investigation; dominance versus submission; type of thematic play engaged in; playing out family routines; and quantity and emotional quality of verbalization.

An example of a study employing children's doll play is one concerned with the effect of father absence on doll play aggression (Sears, Pintler, & Sears, 1946). Sixty-six boys and 60 girls of nursery school age were observed in two 20-minute doll play sessions. Half of the children were from father-absent homes; in most instances the father was in military service. Dolls representing a mother, a father, a preschool-age boy and girl, and a baby were used. The experimenter recorded all instances of aggressive behavior as well as the initiator and the recipient of the aggression. The results showed few differences between the two groups of girls. However, the boys from father-absent homes manifested much less aggression in general than boys from father-present homes. Also, the latter group of boys exhibited much greater aggression toward the father doll, and toward the boy doll. In general, both groups of boys showed more aggression toward the father doll than toward the mother doll.

A recent attempt to study parent-child relations through miniature situations is the one by Santostefano (1962a, b; 1968). In his research, Santostefano has studied both younger and older children, and the parents are involved also in the situation. Four classes of miniature situations have been developed: "in one the mother and the child act upon each other; in a second, mother and child act upon objects for each other; in a third, mother and child act upon objects in each other's presence but not for each other; and lastly, mother and child act upon objects while the other is absent" (1968, p. 298).

The mother and child are presented with a series of two-choice situations and each is asked to choose which he would like to have them play. During the performance of the "task" or situation, questions are asked by the researcher in order to encourage the expression of feelings concerning anxieties, wishes, and attitudes that are usually not directly observable or that cannot be inferred from behavior. "For example, the examiner says to a child, "You asked your mother to give you a drink from a bottle rather than a cup. Tell me about that? Tell me what ideas or feelings you had when you played that game?" Or, "How do you mean you would drink from the bottle but it looks dirty?" (1968, p. 302).

The following are some of the situations included in the four classes: Parent and child act upon each other: child places bracelet on parent, child ties apron on parent, child has parent give him a drink from a bottle or from a cup, parent places bandaid on child. Parent and child act upon objects for each other: parent colors drawing for child, parent tells child a story, child sweeps sawdust with brush for parent. Parent and child act upon objects in eath other's presence: child copies designs accurately, parent finishes interrupted task. Subject (parent or child) acts upon objects with only examiner present: child stands on tall box, parent breaks light bulb.

In an attempt to understand the family dynamics underlying a seven-year-old girl's emotional problems, the child, her sister, and her mother were observed in a series of miniature situations. The following excerpt illustrates some of the kinds of insights which are revealed through this approach:

> Mrs. Z., presented Susan (age 7 years) to a clinic with the complaint that she is doing poorly in school, refuses affection from mother, and is generally immature and a loner.
>
> Mrs. Z. was observed interacting with Susan in a series of miniature situations and in a separate meeting with Helen (Susan's 6-year-old sister), who was reported as functioning adequately.
>
> These sisters made identical choices in several situations which are reported here to illustrate further that the MX technique yields subtle, affective and behavioral responses that nonetheless appear to be psychologically meaningful, easily distinguished, and promising as data for the study of parent-child interaction.
>
> In the situation offering options of guiding mother through a pencil and paper maze (while mother, with eyes closed, held a pencil) or of being guided by mother through the maze, both girls chose to be guided by mother. While guiding Susan, the problem child, mother held the top of the pencil, making no contact with Susan's hand, performed the act stiffly, and did not comment spontaneously. Susan conveyed a serious mood throughout.
>
> With Helen, mother held her hand while guiding her through the maze, smiling and commenting freely, and Helen reciprocated with bursts of laughter. After completing the task, mother spontaneously and enthusiastically noted (apparently associating to the experience of guiding and assisting Helen) that Helen does "A" work in school and that she happened to have brought along a school paper of Helen's. Whereupon she opened her purse and presented the examiner with one of Helen's first grade papers, discussing at some length Helen's consistently above average performance.
>
> In another situation, both girls chose to tie an apron around their mother's waist rather than to place a bracelet on her wrist. When interacting with Susan, mother stood up, and struck what observers described as a model's pose. Susan struggled to reach around mother's

waist in order to tie the apron and mother offered her no assistance. Susan finally was successful in tying the apron, but it sagged well below mother's waistline. Mother commented with an edge of criticism in her tone of voice, "You tied it kind of loose," the only verbal interaction initiated by mother during the situation. When asked why she chose that particular game, Susan offered, "I didn't want to see my mother's pretty dress get dirty."

As Helen attempted to tie the apron around mother's waist, mother gave her assistance by holding the front of the apron. When Helen had tied the apron mother asked playfully, "What would you like me to cook?" and engaged Helen in a brief chat. Later, Helen said she picked the apron game because her mother does a lot of cooking with an apron on. Mother then said to Helen, "You even have an apron of your own, too, don't you," and reported to the examiner that Helen is encouraged to put an apron and help mother with the dishes.

In another situation, Susan chose to have mother give her a drink from a baby's bottle rather than from a cup whereupon mother exclaimed, "Oh Susan, it's been so long!" Regaining her poise, mother picked up the bottle, instructed Susan to put her head back, placed the nipple in Susan's open mouth and squeezed the plastic bottle squirting water in. Observers were impressed by the aggression and absence of warm feeling conveyed by this act. Mother continued squirting water into Susan's mouth until Susan who was obviously uncomfortable and stressed said, "No more." Mother then commented, with humor disguising underlying anger, "Do you want me to burp you too?" Susan did not reply. Immediately after the materials were removed from the table top, mother laughed anxiously, got up and went to her pocketbook, took out a tissue and cleaned her hands.

After Helen made her choice mother patted Helen's forehead gently, and mimicking a mother speaking to an infant said, "Oh my little Helen." Then she placed her hand behind Helen's neck, in a fashion described by observers as "motherly", and put the nipple in Helen's mouth. Helen placed her lips around the nipple. Mother squeezed the bottle and asked, "Is that okay?" When Helen nodded yes, mother proceeded to give her a little more.

(Santostefano, 1968, pp. 305-306)

A final example of a study using a miniature situation is one concerned with analyzing social class differences in maternal teaching styles (Hess & Shipman, 1965). Each mother and her four-year-old child were given several standardized tasks.

In two tasks, the mother was required to explain to her child the simple sorting procedure—for instance, sorting a number of plastic toys by color and by function. The third task required the mother and child to work together to copy five designs on a toy called an Etch-a-Sketch. The mother's language was analyzed on a number of scales, and her approach and effectiveness as a teacher were analyzed in terms of use of praise and criticism as well as the child's degree of success in performing the tasks. Clear social class differences were found with regard to the language scales, particularly on the measure of total verbal output. The better educated mothers tended to use longer sentences, more complex sentences, and a greater number of abstract words than those with less education. The middle class mothers made greater use of praise than the lower class mothers.

The following description of several mothers and their children in the situation where the mother is required to teach the child how to sort a small number of toys clearly illustrates differences among mothers in their teaching styles:

> The first mother outlines the task for the child, gives sufficient help and explanation to permit the child to proceed on her own. She says:
>
> "All right, Susan, this board is the place where we put the little toys; first of all you're supposed to learn how to place them according to color. Can you do that? The things that are all the same color you put in one section; in the second section you put another group of colors, and in the third section you put the last group of colors. Can you do that? Or would you like to see me do it first?"
>
> Child: "I want to do it."
>
> This mother has given explicit information about the task and what is expected of the child; she has offered support and help of various kinds; and she has made it clear that she impelled the child to perform.
>
> A second mother's style offers less clarity and precision. She says in introducing the same task:
>
> "Now, I'll take them all off the board; now you put them all back on the board. What are these?"
>
> Child: "A truck."
>
> "All right, just put them right here; put the other one right here; all right put the other one there."
>
> This mother must rely more on nonverbal communication in her commands; she does not define the task for the child; the child is not

provided with ideas or information that she can grasp in attempting to solve the problem; neither is she told what to expect or what the task is, even in general terms.

A third mother is even less explicit. She introduces the task as follows:

"I've got some chairs and cars, do you want to play the game?" Child does not respond. Mother continues: "O. K. What's this?"

In summary, the miniature situations approach attempts to combine the advantages of naturalistic observation with those obtained by standardizing and controlling the situation. This results in economy of time and effort in that the observer does not have to observe an individual's behavior over a long period of time in order for the behavior under examination to occur. Furthermore, the standard situation permits a ready comparison among children on various dimensions.

Observations 9-12, on pages 89 to 102, illustrate the four approaches discussed on the preceding pages.

SELECTED BIBLIOGRAPHY

Hartshorne, H., & May, M. A. *Studies in the nature of character.* I. *Studies in deceit.* New York: Macmillan, 1928.

Hess, R. D., & Shipman, V. Early experience and the socialization of cognitive modes in children. *Child Development,* 1965, **36**, 869-886.

Jersild, A. T. & Holmes, F. B. Children's fears. *Child Development Monographs,* 1935, No. 20.

Murphy, L. B. *Personality in young children.* Vol. 1. *Methods for the study of personality in young children.* New York: Basic Books, 1956.

Santostefano, S. Miniature situations as a way of interviewing children. *Merrill-Palmer Quarterly,* 1962, **8**, 261-269. (a)

Santostefano, S. Performance testing of personality. *Merrill-Palmer Quarterly,* 1962, **8**, 83-97. (b)

Santostefano, S. Miniature situations and methodological problems in parent-child research. *Merrill-Palmer Quarterly,* 1968, **14**, 285-312.

Sears, R. R., Pintler, M., & Sears, P. S. Effect of father separation on preschool children's doll play aggression. *Child Development,* 1946, **17**, 219-243.

OTHER CHILD STUDY METHODS

Although all methods of obtaining information about children involves observation of one kind or another, most of the methods discussed up to this point have relied on direct observation of the child's behavior. However, there are many important aspects of the child that may not be directly observable. For example, information concerning the child's attitudes toward a variety of issues can best be obtained by questioning him about these issues. A further example, problem-solving ability is extremely important and, while miniature situations have been devised to assess this ability, some aspects of problem solving are verbal in nature and, consequently, verbal or written questionnaires must be used to tap them. Without a doubt, personality is revealed most clearly in everyday behavior; however, in part for reasons of time economy, many personality techniques have been developed that elicit verbal expression. A number of psychometric instruments have been constructed to assess such important intellectual characteristics as reasoning ability, abstract thinking, comprehension, and verbal ability. Finally, in order to understand the child, it is necessary to understand the environment in which he is being reared. For this purpose, interviews with the parents have been employed.

While each of these methods, questionnaires, personality appraisal techniques, psychometric instruments, and interviews possesses advantages and disadvantages, they have all been used extensively to obtain information about children. Each of these will now be discussed in turn.

Questionnaires and Inventories

While straightforward observational approaches are capable of yielding a tremendous amount of information, problems involving quantification of the data, standardization of the situation, comparison across children, and the somewhat cumbersome and time-consuming nature of observation have been discussed. In part for these reasons, as well as for the position that there are some important dimensions that observation alone is unable to tap, standardized questionnaires have been administered to children to get at a variety of intellectual, personality, and attitudinal dimensions, including the following: general information, anxiety, self-concept, need for social approval, perception of parents, internal versus external locus of control, and maturity of moral judgments.

The use of questionnaires has a long history dating back to G. Stanley Hall, an early, eminent psychologist in this country, who, in the late 1800s, became interested in the quantity and quality of information possessed by young children when they enter school. Under Hall's supervision, school teachers in the Boston area administered a general information questionnaire to beginning first grade children. Although such a procedure seems commonplace today, it was a marked contribution at a time when unscientific speculation frequently substituted for the collection of data.

As in the case of any attempt to gain information about broad, partially covert characteristics, one must always be concerned with the adequacy, the reliability, and the validity of the data obtained. For example, in assessing the amount of general information possessed by children of a given age level, the test employed should be broad enough in its coverage to assure an adequate sampling of the area under investigation. With regard to reliability, if children's scores on a test vary greatly from one administration to another, either the characteristic measured by the test is a highly unstable one, or the test itself is unsatisfactory—it is unreliable in terms of measuring the characteristic with any degree of consistency over time. In either case, it is difficult to examine the trait in a meaningful way. Relationships with other variables that might appear to exist at one moment would not hold true later. In a hypothetical example, one might find scores on a test of creativity in children to be closely related to IQ and to a permissive home atmosphere. However, if the test is not reliable, a subsequent administration of the test might reveal no such relation with IQ or home atmosphere.

The issue of the validity of a test is a complex one. Validity is often defined as the extent to which a test measures what it purports to measure—that is, how well does a test measure the characteristic that its author says it measures? Does a test of creativity actually measure creative ability? The validity of early intelligence tests was defined as the extent to which the test scores agreed with teachers' judgments of children's abilities. Tests of the child's learning ability are relatively easy to validate against other stable measures of this area of functioning. Tests of various personality and emotional characteristics are much more difficult to validate, however. There are clear dangers in accepting at face value the validity of a test; the author is obligated to provide such information. Though it may "appear obvious" that a test measures what it claims to measure, this may be highly deceptive. One example should suffice.

Wolff (1946) developed a test to identify the insecure child. Needless to say, the security-insecurity dimension, however defined, has been of great concern to child psychologists. The Wolff Security Test is composed of nine pairs of drawings covering three main concepts: high-low pictures tapping courage versus timidity; protection-alone measuring dependency versus self-sufficiency; and gay-serious assessing mood. The nine pairs of drawings show children in the following situations: 1. Child swinging high-Child swinging low. 2. Child walking on a high fence–Child walking on a low fence. 3. Child high on a ladder–Child almost at the bottom of a ladder. 4. Child jumping off a table by himself–Child being helped off a table by mother. 5. Child playing alone–Child playing with father. 6. Child standing up by himself–Child being helped to stand up by mother. 7. Person smiling–Person not smiling. 8. Children who are friends–Children who are fighting. 9. Child sitting up in bed and bouncing–Child lying quietly in bed.

Since Wolff presented no evidence on the validity of the test (does it agree with other accepted measures of security-insecurity?), another investigator (Martin, 1951) attempted to collect some validity data. The Wolff Security Test was administered to 107 children ranging from three-year-olds to second graders. The children's teachers rated them on two behavior rating scales, the Prichard-Ojemann scale for assessing insecurity in children, and the Haggerty-Olson-Wickman scale measuring maladjustment. In addition, the teachers were asked to nominate the three children they considered most insecure and the three they considered most secure. Martin then computed the extent of agreement among the various measures of insecurity. The results showed that while the two behavior rating scales and the teacher nominations showed significant agreement, none of these measures showed any relation to the scores on the Wolff Security Test. In summary, although the assumptions underlying the Wolff test made sense as did the construction of the test, it did not validly measure what its author set out to measure.

A problem related both to validity and reliability, since it affects these, is that of the veracity of the information that the individual discloses on a questionnaire. How willing is the individual to reveal certain kinds of information and how honest is he in his responses? The ecologists are correct in noting that this problem does not arise when one observes behavior in real-life situations. From an observers point of view, behavior itself cannot be "dishonest" since, at all times, it reveals important kinds of information about an individual. With questionnaires, on the other hand, distortion, for whatever reason, frequently is present. While distortion or falsification may be deliberate, it may just as likely be unconscious. The extent to which distortion occurs on a questionnaire is related to the sensitivity of a particular area for a given individual. Little distortion may be present on questionnaires dealing with factual information such as that elicited by G. Stanley Hall from preschool children. However, questionnaires tapping various personality dimensions may be much more susceptible to distortion. Moreover, individuals differ greatly in their areas of sensitivity, and, too, it is difficult to assess the extent of falsification or distortion present. Much of our present discussion is relevant also to the interview method which will be discussed later.

In summary, the questionnaire method possesses several advantages and disadvantages. A great amount of data can be collected in a brief period of time from a large number of children. This enables the investigator to make a variety of comparisons: age and sex differences, social class differences, etc. Also, responses on the questionnaire may be related to other intellectual and personality variables, such as the relation between amount of information possessed by a child and his academic success in school, or the relation between anxiety and creativity. Furthermore some of the information elicited by questionnaires is not directly observable, such as the parent's attitudes toward childrearing or the child's moral judgments concerning the relative seriousness of various offenses.

The disadvantages of questionnaires revolve mainly around the issue of veracity as well as the willingness of the individual to divulge certain kinds of information. Finally, it might be argued that an individual's attitude toward an issue may be less important than his behavior when confronted with a situation involving that issue. For example, a parent's attitude toward childrearing may affect the child less than the parent's behavior toward the child.

Observation 13, which involves administering a preschool information questionnaire, illustrates the questionnaire approach to collecting information about children.

SELECTED BIBLIOGRAPHY

Hall, G. S. The contents of children's minds. *Princeton Review,* 1883, 249-272. Reprinted in W. Dennis (Ed.), *Readings in the history of psychology.* New York: Appleton, 1948. Pp. 255-276.

Martin, W. E. Identifying the insecure child: I. The Wolff Security Test. *Journal of Genetic Psychology,* 1951, **78**, 217-232.

Medinnus, G. R. An investigation of school readiness. Unpublished manuscript, 1959.

Probst, G. A. A general information test for kindergarten children. *Child Development,* 1931, **2**, 81-95.

Templin, M. C. General information of kindergarten children, a comparison with the Probst study after 26 years. *Child Development,* 1958, **29**, 87-96.

Wolff, W. *The personality of the preschool child.* New York: Grune & Stratton, 1946.

Personality Appraisal Techniques and Psychometric Tests of Ability

Techniques for assessing personality and intellectual ability are similar in the sense that they both involve observing and recording the child's behavior and responses in situations in which he is presented with various materials and tasks. Specific instructions are given the child with regard to what is expected of him. These techniques might be considered shorthand methods of observation in that their intent is to obtain a great deal of information in a short period of time. Moreover, the instruments are designed to probe into significant areas of functioning so that the information obtained is highly critical in understanding the child.

For a great many reasons, tests of ability are more precise, more highly developed, and more accurate in predicting other kinds of behaviors (e.g., school achievement) than are personality measures. Important here is the fact that, as compared with personality, intelligence can be defined more narrowly and with greater precision. Other definition of personality is ambiguous, amorphous, and complex. Attempts to predict adult adjustment, however defined, from earlier behaviors have not been highly successful. Mention might be made also of the notion that behavior may be situation-specific. A child may cheat in one situation but not in another, in which case it is inappropriate to speak of a general trait of honesty. Furthermore, various life experiences alter behavior and attitudes. A child may be anxious and aggressive at one point; however, these characteristics are subject to modification by subsequent experiences. Finally, factors comprising intellectual ability may be more stable in nature than those involved in personality. While temporary moods and attitudes affect, to some extent, a child's performance on an IQ test, they play a much larger role in his responses to personality measures. This leads to low reliability over time on these measures.

Observation 14, on pages 107 to 110, provides the student with experience in administering and evaluating either a projective test or a psychometric test of intellectual functioning.

Personality Appraisal Techniques

In addition to the observational methods and the questionnaire and inventory type measures of personality already discussed, many other techniques have been developed. While a number of these have been based on tests designed originally for adults, others have been developed specifically for the child level. Also, some tests have grown out of specific theories of personality and personality development. Others simply represent attempts to elicit various kinds of information from the child concerning his attitudes, motives, and behavior tendencies. Most personality measures are based on the assumption that, in his responses, the child will unwittingly reveal significant aspects of his psychological makeup.

Varying along a structured to unstructured dimension, personality appraisal techniques may be divided into two broad categories depending on whether or not a verbal response is required of the child.

Included in the verbal response category are word association tests, sentence completion tests, and techniques in which the child is asked to tell a story about a picture. The most common of the nonverbal methods, sometimes called expressive or productive techniques, involves children's drawings, usually of human figures. In both the verbal and the nonverbal techniques the investigator interprets the child's responses in terms of broad psychological dimensions and behavior dynamics. Primarily these techniques are employed as clinical tools to gain an understanding of an individual child. Norms for various age and sex groups are seldom available.

Figure 2 is a sample picture from a test designed to assess the child's relationship with his parents (Alexander, 1955). The child is asked to compose a story about the picture, describing what led up to the scene depicted, what is occurring, and what the outcome will be. The stories are evaluated in terms of their emotional content, whether positive or negative, and the way in which the characters are viewed, whether friendly or hostile.

FIGURE 2. Sample picture from the Alexander Adult-Child Interaction Test (Alexander, 1952).

Sometimes the pictures used are more structured in nature, eliciting a fairly narrow range of responses. Figure 3 is drawn from a series of pictures designed to assess characteristics of punishment responses in the mother-child relationship (Morgan & Gaier, 1956). Using the scoring factors developed by Rosenzweig in his Picture Frustration Test, the children's stories are scored for three types of reaction in a punishment situation:

FIGURE 3. Card 6 of the Male Series of the Punishment Situation Index dealing with the lack of neatness in personal habits (Morgan & Gaier, 1956).

obstacle-dominance in which the barrier causing the frustration is emphasized; ego-defense in which the ego of the subject predominates; and need-persistence in which the solution to the frustrating problem is emphasized.

The following are the sentence stems comprising a sentence completion test designed to assess several aspects of the parent-child relationship (Hoeflin & Kell, 1959). The child's responses are scored on the basis of how he conceives of the parent and child roles; general positiveness or negativeness of feeling is also noted.

1. Our family
2. As a child I enjoyed
3. My mother
4. Being a child
5. Obedience
6. Children should not
7. If my father
8. When I was in high school
9. I wish my parents had
10. Being a (boy) (girl)
11. Discipline
12. Teen-agers
13. My father
14. Making high grades in school
15. Punishment
16. As a child I disliked
17. A democratic family
18. If my mother

19. Being at home
20. Making decisions in the home

Interpretations of children's drawings and paintings has a long history. However, attempts to develop objective criteria for scoring these products have been largely unsuccessful. Consequently, they must be considered primarily as clinical tools for observing an individual child's behavior—how he approaches a task; whether he is tense or relaxed; random comments made while absorbed in a task; and a variety of other behavioral dimensions.

If the personality assessment techniques discussed briefly in this section were to be judged on the basis of (a) how closely they agree with longer samples of direct observation of behavior, and (b) their utility in adding to our knowledge about a child, we would have to conclude that their accomplishments are not impressive. Clearly, however, the more situations in which we observe a child, the more we learn about him, and some children reveal more about themselves in one situation than in another. On the whole, some of the observational techniques described earlier appear more useful in child study in terms of the quality and quantity of information obtained than the several verbal and nonverbal techniques described here.

Psychometric Tests Of Intelligence

At a time when intelligence tests and the uses made of them are subjected to an increasing amount of criticism from many sources, it might be easy to dismiss them as biased, unfair, and meaningless. To some extent the criticism is justified, and it has caused us to re-examine the entire concept of intelligence, its measurement, and the uses made of intelligence test scores. Clearly, intelligence, no matter how defined, must be viewed as only one of many important aspects of the developing child. A very brief historical account of the development of intelligence tests may help to place them in proper perspective.

Prior to the development of IQ tests as we now know them, psychologists were interested in assessing individual differences in a variety of specific behaviors thought to be related to intellectual ability. Most of the measures explored were laboratory-type tests of a sensorimotor nature. These included tests of reaction time, muscular strength, keenness of hearing and vision, and discrimination of weight. However, these measures of relatively simple psychophysical functions did not correlate with such measures of intellectual functioning as school grades and teachers' ratings of intellectual ability.

Attempts by Binet and his co-workers to assess complex intellectual functions became focalized in 1904 when the French Minister of Public Instruction appointed a commission to study the development of methods for identifying and educating children who could not profit from instruction in the public classroom. The early Binet-Simon scale resulted from this effort. Based on their definition of intelligence, the test included measures of comprehension, reasoning, and judgment, with abstract verbal ability playing an important role. While the original test has undergone a number of translations and revisions, it remains the most widely used individually administered test of intelligence.

Several reasons account for the wide popularity and great usage of the Binet test, known in this country as the Stanford-Binet because of its translation under the direction of Lewis M. Terman at Stanford University. First, the test was a highly reliable measuring instrument; periodic tests administered over varying time intervals showed high agreement. Second, the test predicted, with fair accuracy, a child's school achievement. In retrospect, it can be said that the peak of intelligence testing was reached in the 1950s. Concern has now shifted to an interest in developing measures of specific areas of functioning and of specific areas of learning disability.

A great many issues and a great many correlates of intelligence have been examined as a result of the construction of a reliable and valid measuring instrument. Among them are: Is one's intellectual ability due primarily to heredity or to environment? Is IQ fixed at birth or does it change over time? Can education raise a person's IQ? Are there racial and social class differences in IQ? Is there a relation between IQ and general life adjustment?

A variety of measures of ability are available today. They include individually-administered and group-administered tests; tests of infant development; nonverbal tests; and "culture-free" or "culture-fair" tests. Each of these tests is composed of a number of items tapping many different intellectual functions or abilities: memory, deductive reasoning, analogical thinking, vocabulary, spatial orientation, and perceptual discrimination. Each of the individual items has undergone a great deal of refinement and has been subjected to careful examination in terms of (1) the extent to which the child's performance on that item agrees with his performance on the test as a whole, (2) the precise manner of presenting the task to the child, and (3) the exact manner of scoring the child's performance. Furthermore, psychometric tests of ability are carefully standardized, with norms on various subpopulations of children. Thus, the performance of a six-year-old girl, for example, can be compared with other six-year-olds, and her score can be interpreted on that basis. It is for all of these reasons that psychometric tests provide a very distilled sample of behavior that, although of short duration, reflects with fair accuracy the child's general level of intellectual functioning.

In addition to observing the child's performance on individual test items and interpreting his total score, observation of a number of other test behavior variables furnishes further information about the child. Scales for rating such test behaviors accompany most IQ tests. For example, four behaviors are rated on the Stanford-Binet IQ test: willingness, self-confidence, social confidence, and attention. Test behavior during the administration of the Peabody Picture Vocabulary Test is rated on these variables: rapport, guessing, speed of response, verbalization, attention span, perseveration, and need for praise. Judgments on other characteristics are also made; these include motor activity, amount of sedation, ambulation, speech, hearing, and vision.

In summary, psychometric tests are the most highly developed, highly sophisticated instruments we have for assessing the child's present level of intellectual functioning. They are highly reliable. They are valid in the sense that scores on these tests agree with other estimates of intellectual ability, and they predict school achievement, the purpose for which they were originally designed. However, a great many factors in the test situation affect the child's performance, such as motivation, rapport between child and examiner, physical health, momentary mood, attention, and the child's familiarity with a situation in which the child is sitting face-to-face with an adult who plies him with questions to which he is expected to respond. For these and many other reasons IQ scores should be viewed with caution; they should be interpreted and used wisely; and they must never be seen as immutable devices for pigeonholing or labeling a child.

SELECTED BIBLIOGRAPHY

Alexander, T. The Adult-Child Interaction Test. *Monographs of the Society for Research in Child Development,* 1952, **17**, No. 2.

Bronfenbrenner, U., & Ricciuti, H. The appraisal of personality characteristics in children. In P. Mussen (Ed.), *Handbook of research methods in child development.* New York: Wiley, 1960. Pp. 770–817.

Goodenough, F. L. *Measurement of intelligence by drawings.* Tarrytown-on-Hudson, N.Y.: World Book, 1926.

Henry, W. Projective techniques. In P. Mussen (Ed.), *Handbook of research methods in child development.* New York: Wiley, 1960, Pp. 603–644.

Hoeflin, R., & Kell, L. The Kell-Hoeflin Incomplete Sentences Blank: Youth-Parent Relations. *Monographs of the Society for Research in Child Development,* 1959, **24**, No. 3.

Morgan, P., & Gaier, E. Types of reactions in punishment situations in the mother-child relationship. *Child Development,* 1957, **28**, 161–166.

Interview Method

Although the interview has been used primarily as a clinical tool for understanding an individual child, it has been used fairly extensively in research as well. The area of research in which it has been employed most frequently is that of parent-child relations. An interview schedule is developed to elicit information from the parents on a number of psychological dimensions. Typically rating scales are used in conjunction with the interview in order to quantify the material obtained in the interview.

Although interviews have been used with children, their use here has been limited, and usually interviews have been combined with other methods such as doll play or projective techniques in which the child tells a story about a picture. Problems of language and communication make the straightforward question and answer type of interview difficult with children. The present discussion will be limited to interviews with parents.

An interview may be totally unplanned, in which the interviewee is free to pursue any topic he wishes, or it may be confined to a predetermined list of questions. Each type has its advantages and disadvantages and, in actual practice, the interview is seldom completely one or the other. Frequently in the initial stages of an interview, rapport is established by letting the parent discuss areas that he selects; later the interviewer may wish to dig further into certain points or to obtain information where gaps exist.

An early, extensive research project designed to assess the atmosphere of the home was conducted at the Fels Research Institute in Yellow Springs, Ohio. The mothers of the children participating in the longitudinal study were interviewed in their homes at six month intervals. The mother's interaction with her children was also casually observed. Following each interview, the investigator rated the home on 30 scales representing psychological dimensions thought to be important in influencing the child's development. Figures 4 and 5 are examples of the Fels Parent Behavior Rating Scales. Unfortunately, the Fels researchers have never published their interview schedule nor excerpts from their interviews so it is difficult to determine the basis for the ratings.

The interrelations among the 30 scales have been examined, and three main syndromes or clusters have emerged: Acceptance of the Child, Democracy in the Home, and Indulgence. Any given home may be classified by a combination of these three factors. For example, an acceptant home might be rated high also on democracy and indulgence. In a further refinement of the Acceptance cluster, two types of rejecting homes were distinguished: nonchalant and actively rejecting. In the nonchalant home, the child was largely ignored but was punished severely for infractions or disturbances. In the actively rejecting homes that were also autocratic, the demand for compliance reduced the opportunity for disturbance.

In addition to identifying the significant psychological dimensions in the home, the Fels researchers have sought to establish relationships between the home atmosphere and the child's behavior in nursery school and in elementary school. The children in their sample were observed at some length and their behavior rated on a number of variables. In the preschool years, the actively rejected children were characterized by high emotionality and low emotional control. They showed resistance to adults and were more active physically than accepted children. Children from indulgent homes were high on both friendliness and quarrelsomeness. At school age, indulged children seemed shyer and less sociable than during preschool years, while rejected children showed a marked increase in quarrelsomeness and a great deal of hostility toward siblings. Children from democratic homes showed increases in IQ over a period of time, due in part to the fact that democratic homes permit and encourage curiosity, exploration, and experimentation. On such intellectual variables as planfulness, curiosity, and originality the democratically reared children rated high. In nursery school these youngsters were active, aggressive, fearless, likely to be leaders, somewhat cruel, nonconformist, and disobedient. Although strict control in the home tended to reduce disobedience, quarrelsomeness, and negativism, it also decreased fearlessness, planfulness, tenacity, and aggressiveness. Taken together, these qualities seemed to describe a well-behaved child but one characterized by a constricted personality.

The book, *Patterns of Child Rearing* (Sears, Maccoby, & Levin, 1957), describes another large-scale study employing maternal interviews. Mothers of 379 kindergarten children

FELS PARENT BEHAVIOR RATING SCALE NO. 7.2

Acceptance of Child
(Devotion—Rejection)

Serial Sheet No.

1	2	3	4	5	6	7	8	9	10	Number
										Period of observation
										Ratee
										Age in
										Months at End of Period
										Child

Rate the parent's acceptance of the child into his own inner circle of loyalty and devotion. Does the parent act in such a way as to indicate that the child is considered an intimate and inseparable partner? Or does the parent act as though he resents the child's intrusion and rejects the child's bid for a place in his primary area of devotion?

Consider all evidence which in any way may impinge upon the child as acceptance—rejection, however subtle, vague, or indirect. It is not the parent's true feeling, but his attitude, as a functioning unit in the child's environment, which we are rating.

— Parent's behavior toward child connotes utter devotion and acceptance into his innermost self, without stint or suggestion of holding back in any phase of his life.

— Parents clearly accepts child. Includes child in family councils, trips, affection, even when it is difficult or represents considerable sacrifice.

— A "Charter member" of the family but "kept in his place". Parent accepts child in general, but excludes him from certain phases of parent's life.

— Tacit acceptance. Excludes child so frequently that to the child the rejection attitude may seem to predominate even though parent takes acceptance for granted.

— Parent's predominant tendency is to avoid, repulse, and exclude the child, but without open rejection.

— Child openly resented and rejected by parent. Never admitted to inner circle. Made to feel unwanted, ostracized

										Score
										Tolerance
										Range
1	2	3	4	5	6	7	8	9	10	Number

Rater:	Date of Rating:
Scored by:	Date:
Checked by:	Date:
Tabulated by:	Date:

Rater's Remarks: (continue on back of sheet)

FIGURE 4.

FELS PARENT BEHAVIOR RATING SCALE NO. 3.15

Democracy of Regulation and Enforcement Policy (Democratic—Dictatorial)

Serial Sheet No.

1	2	3	4	5	6	7	8	9	10	Number
										Period of observation
										Ratee
										Age in
										Months at End of Period
										Child

Rate the parent's tendency to share with the child the formulation of regulations for the child's conduct. Does the parent give the child a voice in determining what the policy shall be? Or does the parent hand down the established policy from above?

Disregard immediate issues not covered by policy (See Coerciveness of Suggestion). Rate independent of justification of policy to child, and independent of restrictiveness of regulations. Include both overt consulting with child and considering child's expressed wishes. Dictatorial policies may be wise or foolish, benevolent or selfish.

— Endures much inconvenience and some risk to child's welfare in giving child large share in policy forming. Consults with child in formulating policies whenever possible.

— Attempts to adjust policies to child's wishes wherever practicable. Often consults child.

— Deliberately democratic in certain safe or trivial matters, but dictates when there is a sharp conflict between child's wishes and other essential requirements.

— Neither democratic nor dictatorial, deliberately. Follows most practical or easiest course in most cases.

— Tends to be rather dictatorial but usually gives benevolent consideration to child's desires. Seldom consults child.

— Dictatorial in most matters, but accedes to child's wishes occasionally when they do not conflict with own convenience or standards.

— Dictates policies without regard to child's wishes. Never consults child when setting up regulations.

										Score
										Tolerance
										Range
1	2	3	4	5	6	7	8	9	10	Number

Rater:	Date of Rating:
Scored by: Checked by: Tabulated by:	Date: Date: Date:

Rater's Remarks: (continue on back of sheet)

FIGURE 5.

were interviewed concerning three main questions: First, how do parents rear their children? Second, what effects do different kinds of training have on children? Third, what leads a mother to use one method rather than another?

An extensive interview schedule was constructed to elicit information about dimensions the researchers deemed pertinent. Some of the main areas of childrearing that the interviews dealt with were feeding, toilet training, dependency, sex, aggression, restrictions and demands, techniques of training, and the development of conscience.

In order to try to eliminate stereotyped answers and to avoid distortions, several devices were used in wording the questions:

1. (Face saving) "Do you ever find time to play with Johnny just for your own pleasure?" (instead of "Do you ever play ... ")

2. (Assuming the existence of negatively valued behavior) "In what ways do you get on each other's nerves?" (instead of "Do you ever get on each other's nerves?")

3. (Making a wide range of answers appear socially acceptable) "Some people feel it's very important for a child to learn not to fight with other children, and other people feel there are times when a child has to learn to fight. How do you feel about this?"

4. (Pitting two stereotypes-values-against each other) "Do you keep track of exactly where Johnny is and what he is doing most of the time, or can you let him watch out for himself quite a bit?" (Here the value of being a careful mother, who protects her child from danger, is pitted against the value of training a child to be independent.)

(pp. 21)

Following the taping of the interviews and transcribing them, the typed records were rated on 188 scales, ranging from "amount of caretaking in infancy by mother" to "husband's reaction to wife's pregnancy."

Mother: I don't know. I love little babies. I love to do with little babies. I love to teach them things. I think it's a feather in your cap to see a little baby be able to do something and know that you taught them that, but at the same time, I think they are interesting when they grow up, too. I found them interesting all the way along. I just love kids.

Mother: Well, if I had been well and a little younger, I might have enjoyed him, but I will say frankly that it was just a hard job for me. (pp. 51 and 52)

Interestingly, factor analysis, which involves identifying the main dimensions underlying a number of related measures, of the scales on which the interviews in the Pattern study were rated, revealed factors similar to those found in the Fels research. Moreover, these same factors have appeared with regularity in other parent-child research; consequently, these two factors would appear to be the major ones in describing the psychological atmosphere of the home: acceptance-rejection (or love-hostility) and autocratic-democratic (or control-autonomy).

The interview method has been open to criticism because of the distortions that may be present in the parent's verbal report. These distortions may be either deliberate or unconscious. Some problems of communication between interviewer and parent add to the difficulty. Questions may be misunderstood or misinterpreted, and the definition of specific words may be unclear. Several approaches have been used to minimize distortion. Hoffman (1957) has asked the parent to report in great detail everything that occurred between him and his child the day preceding the interview. Hoffman reasoned that the sheer task of recalling events in such detail tended to become so absorbing that personal involvement in the events diminished. Another approach has been to interview different members of the same family separately, thus attempting to identify significant discrepancies. Some research has even used relatives and friends as informants.

Retrospective falsification presents another cause for concern with information obtained through interviews. The passage of time may result in distortion and selective forgetting. Memory is seldom completely accurate. In the Pattern study, for example, the mothers were asked questions pertaining to events and attitudes prior to the child's birth as well as a number of other questions dealing with factual and attitudinal information from birth to the time of the interview when the child was five years old. Not only is it likely that retrospective falsification occurred in their reports, but worse, it is nearly impossible to determine to what extent selective forgetting occurred and in which areas it was most marked.

A number of methodological studies have been conducted to identify the precise nature of retrospective falsification in interviews with parents. One study (Haggard, Brekstad, & Skard, 1960) interviewed mothers four times over a period beginning about a month before delivery and ending when the child was between seven and eight years of age. In general, the final interviews were more a reflection of the mother's current recollections of the past than an accurate account of past events. The accuracy of recall was associated with the type of information requested. Specific facts, such as the length of the child at birth, were recalled best, whereas information on general wishes and attitudes were recalled next best. Earlier anxieties of the mother were recalled least accurately.

Mothers vary greatly on a number of dimensions that affect their reporting in an interview situation and, while these differences may reveal a fair amount about the mother as a person, they may cloud the interviewer's impression of the mother's relation with her children. For example, a mother with a strong need for social approval may portray events in a manner that is quite at variance with the facts. And, although facts as such, the mother's reporting of the facts, and the mother's attitudes toward these facts, are all important kinds of information, it is difficult to sort out these various factors.

The parent interview will remain an important source of information about many aspects of the child's day-to-day behavior and about possible causes of this behavior resting in the family situation: the relation between the parents; their attitudes and behavior toward the child; the child's perception of these; and the child's relationships with his sibling. Precautions must be taken with regard to the interpretation of data obtained through interviews. Successful interviewing requires an enormous amount of training, experience, and skill.

The interview questions included in Observation 15, on pages 112 to 114, provide the student with experience in conducting and evaluating the interview method in collecting information about the home environment of children.

SELECTED BIBLIOGRAPHY

Baldwin, A. L. The effect of home environment on nursery school behavior. *Child Development,* 1949, **20**, 49-61.

Baldwin, A. L., Kalhorn, J., & Breese, F. Patterns of parent behavior. *Psychological Monographs,* 1945, **58**, No. 3.

Baldwin, A. L., Kalhorn, J., & Breese, F. The appraisal of parent behavior. *Psychological Monographs,* 1949, **63**, No. 4.

Haggard, E. A., Brekstad, A., & Skard, A. On the reliability of the anamnestic interview. *Journal of Abnormal and Social Psychology,* 1960, **61**, 311-318.

Hoffman, M. L. An interview method for obtaining descriptions of parent-child interaction. *Merrill-Palmer Quarterly,* 1957, **4**, 76-83.

Yarrow, L. Interviewing children. In P. Mussen (Ed.), *Handbook of research methods in child development.* New York: Wiley, 1960. Pp. 561-602.

Section B

Observations

Observation 1

Naturalistic Observation of an Infant

Observe a young child under the age of two. Record in longhand everything that you observe of his ongoing behavior during a 5 to 10 minute time period. Choose a time when the infant is playing by himself in order to simplify this initial observation. When you have completed the observation, answer the following questions:

1. To what extent do you feel you were able to record *all* of the behavior? What behaviors might you have missed or omitted, while concentrating on others? What might have caused some of these possible biases in what you, as an observer, chose to record?
2. Do you feel your observation was very specific and detailed or fairly general? For example, were you able to describe precisely the nature of the infant's motor movements or were your descriptions stated in general terms regarding gross motor activity? Another example, were you able to pinpoint the vowels and consonants the infant used in his vocalizations or did you simply note that the infant made sounds?

3. To what extent do you feel your present vocabulary is adequate to describe an infant's behavior? Give examples.
4. What things did you learn about a child's behavior from observing it and recording it that you did not know before?
5. From this observation alone, were you able to draw any conclusions about the child's development in a variety of areas relative to that expected of his age level? How do you think he compares with an average child his age?
6. Do you feel that the fact that you were observing the infant altered his behavior in any way? How? What might you have done to avoid this?

Observation 2

Inter-Observer Agreement

Repeat Observation 1 using a different child. Use two observers recording the behavior simultaneously with no prior discussion of any aspect of the observation. Following the observation, compare the two records on these points:

1. To what extent were the two observers looking at the same kinds of behavior? For example, did one emphasize motor behavior more than another? If so, why might this have been the case? Was one observer's description more general in nature; in other words, were the two observers describing different levels of behavior? For example, one observer may have described with some precision the way in which an infant grasped an object while the other dealt with more general aspects of behavior.
2. Attempt to "score" the records for the main behaviors noted—such as, "child picked up a block" and "stuck

it in his mouth." Inter-rater agreement can be specified in a percentage figure using this formula:

$$\frac{\text{Number of agreements}}{\text{Number of agreements + number of disagreements}} \times 100$$

In determining this percentage for your records, number of agreements would be the number of specific behaviors recorded by both observers while the number of disagreements would be the number of behaviors that one observer recorded and the other did not.

3. What kind of "training" might have preceded the observation to increase inter-observer agreement?
4. What did you learn about characteristics of children, child behavior, observation of children, and the problems of agreement between observers from this observation?

Observation 3

Description of a Single Child

Observe a four- to six-year-old child in a free-play situation for approximately one hour. Describe everything you can about the child: his physical appearance, his behavior, any observable characteristic. The purpose of this observation is not to keep a running account of a child's ongoing behavior, but rather to record your impressions of a child from observing him. The first part of your report should be a straightforward description of the child. In the second part, attempt to draw some conclusions about the child's personality based on your observation of his behavior. For this purpose, draw a line dividing your paper in half, with the descriptions of the child's behavior on the left, and your interpretations of the personality characteristics these behaviors seem to indicate on the right. For example:

C. (child) went from one group of children to another, interfering with or disrupting their activities.	C. has a high need for social approval but so far has not learned socially acceptable ways of obtaining this approval.

DISCUSSION

1. In what ways are a description of a child's behavior and an interpretation of that behavior different? How do observer biasses affect these two records?
2. What were some aspects of behavior that you felt you were unable to interpret? Why?
3. In what other situations would you like to observe the child in order to draw firmer conclusions about various aspects of his behavior?
4. What did you learn about child observation and child behavior from this observation?

Observation 4

Age Differences in Child Behavior

Observe two groups of children separately, for approximately one hour each in free play situations. Choose one group of preschool age (three- to five-year-olds) and the other of elementary school age (second or third grade). Again, as in Observation 3, do not attempt to record ongoing behavior as an ecologist would, but rather, record your description of various child characteristics at the two age levels and the children's behavior. The purpose of this observation is to sharpen your powers of observation by focusing on specific aspects of behavior, describing them in some detail, and by contrasting two different age levels on these behaviors. Following your observational recordings, report your observations on a sheet divided in half, with the observation of one age level on the left and the other on the right, with similar aspects of behavior opposite each other. For example:

Time of observations: ________________ ________________

Number of children in group: ________________ ________________

Four-year-olds:	*Third graders:*
Social behavior	
The children spent most of their time running about in rather unorganized play. Social groupings were transient and the duration of a single play episode was short.	Most of the hour was spent in organized play, with the sexes largely segregated. Two different groups of four boys each spent the entire period playing tether ball while the girls played, with a great deal of skill and coordination, hopscotch and jump rope.

If possible, note specific aspects of each of the following areas:

1. Motor coordination.
2. Size of groupings.
3. Duration of groupings.
4. Complexity of play activities.
5. Proportion of time spent in active play versus more sedentary activities.
6. Leader-follower relationships.
7. Harmonious, cooperative interactions versus quarreling and conflicts.
8. Friendship patterns.
9. Sex differences.
10. Emotional reactions to frustration, thwarting, aggression, rejection.

DISCUSSION

1. Attempt to draw some conclusions about age differences in a number of areas and use these conclusions to explain differences in behavior. For example, age differences between four-year-olds and third graders in motor coordination and attention span help to explain differences in the kinds and duration of activities.
2. What were some of the age differences that impressed you most?
3. In what areas of development did you observe the greatest age differences?
4. What did you learn from this observation?

Observation 5

Identifying Age Levels

Perhaps one of the best and most interesting ways for a person to discover how knowledgeable he is about the facts of child behavior and development is to attempt to estimate the ages of children he meets casually in everyday life. Accuracy requires keen and perceptive observation of specific aspects of the child's physical appearance and behavior. For example, what does a two-year-old look like? What are some of the things he can and cannot do? What are some of his characteristic activities? How does he differ from a one-year-old and from a three-year old? In order to answer these questions, one must be highly familiar with a great many developmental norms that describe typical behaviors at different age levels. While there is a wide range among normal children in the age at which various behaviors appear, development is so rapid in the early years that six months of chronological age is sufficient to produce marked differences in behavior. For example, few, if any, six-month-olds can walk alone while many twelve-month-old infants are able to do so. In the later preschool years, as the rate of development slows down, larger age differences are required in order for one to distinguish accurately between age levels.

Broad knowledge of normal behavior and development permits one to identify abnormalities of development. The concern of many parents with their child's development might be eliminated if they knew what behavior to expect of a child at a given age level. This is why parents are often asked to observe their child in a group of children similar in age in a nursery school or classroom situation. Also, discussions among parents serve to provide information about normal patterns of development.

Before attempting to estimate the ages of children, become thoroughly familiar with the contents of Tables 1 to 4. Next, observe one child at each of the following age levels: 6 months, 12 months, 18 months, 2 years, 3 years, 4 years, five years, 6 years, and 7 years. Do not record ongoing behavior as you have done in some of the previous observations. Rather, list developmental behaviors and characteristics that reflect the child's age level, based in part on the information contained in the accompanying Tables. While some of these behaviors require administering a specific task to the child and observing his response, others can be observed in the child's undirected activities. In observing a 12 month-old child, for example, you might look at his (a) general physical size and proportions; (b) gross motor behavior in terms of ability to walk, whether alone, with assistance, or by holding on to furniture; (c) fine motor ability in terms of picking up and holding objects; (d) language ability; and (e) feeding behavior. You need not spend a great deal of time observing a child at each of the age levels, but enough so that you are reasonably certain of some of the distinguishing characteristics.

To complete the present observational assignment, select 5 children that you encounter at random in a store or at a playground, for instance. Attempt to determine their ages based on your noting and listing specific age-related behavioral characteristics. Following this, ask the child, or the adult with the child, the child's chronological age.

TABLE 1. Developmental Milestones in Motor and Language Development[a]

At the completion of:	*Motor Development*	*Vocalization and Language*
12 weeks	Supports head when in prone position; weight is on elbows; hands mostly open; no grasp reflex	Markedly less crying than at 8 weeks; when talked to and nodded at, smiles, followed by squealing-gurgling sounds usually called *cooing,* which is vowel-like in character and pitch-modulated; sustains cooing for 15-20 seconds
16 weeks	Plays with a rattle placed in his hands (by shaking it and staring at it), head self-supported; tonic neck reflex subsiding.	Responds to human sounds more definitely; turns head; eyes seem to search for speaker; occasionally some chuckling sounds
20 weeks	Sits with props	The vowel-like cooing sounds begin to be interspersed with more consonantal-sounds; labial fricatives, spirants and nasals are common; acoustically, all vocalizations are very different from the sounds of the mature language of the environment
6 months	Sitting: bends forward and uses hands for support; can bear weight when put into standing position, but cannot yet stand with holding on; reaching: unilateral; grasp: no thumb apposition yet; releases cube when given another	Cooing changing into babbling resembling one-syllable utterances; neither vowels nor consonants have very fixed recurrences; most common utterances sound somewhat like ma, mu, da, or di
8 months	Stands holding on; grasps with thumb apposition; picks up pellet with thumb and finger tips	Reduplication (or more continuous repetitions) becomes frequent; intonation patterns become distinct; utterances can signal emphasis and emotions

TABLE 1. *(Continued)*

At the completion of:	*Motor Development*	*Vocalization and Language*
10 months	Creeps efficiently; takes side-steps, holding on; pulls to standing position	Vocalizations are mixed with sound-play such as gurgling or bubble-blowing; appears to wish to imitate sounds, but the imitations are never quite successful; beginning to differentiate between words heard by making differential adjustment
12 months	Walks when held by one hand; walks on feet and hands—knees in air; mouthing of objects almost stopped; seats self on floor	Identical sound sequences are replicated with higher relative frequency of occurrence and words (mama or dadda) are emerging; definite signs of understanding some words and simple commands (show me your eyes)
18 months	Grasp, prehension and release fully developed; gait stiff propulsive and precipitated; sits on child's chair with only fair aim; creeps downstairs backward; has difficulty building tower of 3 cubes	Has a definite repertoire of words—more than three, but less than fifty; still much babbling but now of several syllables with intricate intonation pattern; no attempt at communicating information and no frustration for not being understood; words may include items such as thank you or come here, but there is little ability to join any of the lexical items into spontaneous two-item phrases; understanding is progressing rapidly
24 months	Runs, but falls in sudden turns; can quickly alternate between sitting and stance; walks stairs up or down,	Vocabulary of more than 50 items (some children seem to be able to name everything in environ-

	one foot forward only	ment); begins spontaneously to join vocabulary items into two-word phrases; all phrases appear to be own creations; definite increase in communicative behavior and interest in language
30 months	Jumps up into air with both feet; stands on one foot for about two seconds; takes few steps on tip-toe; jumps from chair; good hand and finger coordination; can move digits independently; manipulation of objects much improved; builds tower of six cubes	Fastest increase in vocabulary with many new additions every day; no babbling at all; utterances have communicative intent; frustrated if not understood by adults; utterances consist of at least two words, many have three or even five words; sentences and phrases have characteristic child grammar, that is, they are rarely verbatim repetitions of an adult utterance; intelligibility is not very good yet, though there is great variation among children; seems to understand everything that is said to him
3 years	Tiptoes three yards; runs smoothly with acceleration and deceleration; negotiates sharp and fast curves without difficulty; walks stairs by alternating feet; jumps 12 inches; can operate tricycle	Vocabulary of some 1000 words; about 80% of utterances are intelligible even to strangers; grammatical complexity of utterances is roughly that of colloquial adult language, although mistakes still occur
4 years	Jumps over rope; hops on right foot; catches ball in arms; walks line	Language is well-established; deviations from the adult norm tend to be more in style than in grammar

[a] *Source.* Lenneberg, E. H. *Biological Foundations of Language.* New York: Wiley, 1967. Pp. 128–130.

TABLE 2. Developmental Sequences in Four Areas of Behavior[a]

Age Level	*Developmental Area*			
	Motor Behavior	*Adaptive Behavior*	*Language Behavior*	*Personal-Social Behavior*
5 years	Skips on alternate feet	Counts 10 pennies	Speaks without infantile articulation. Asks "Why?"	Dresses without assistance. Asks meanings of words
4 years	Skips on one foot	Builds gate of 5 cubes. Draws "man"	Uses conjunctions. Understands prepositions	Can wash and dry face. Goes on errands. Plays cooperatively
3 years	Stands on one foot. Builds tower of 10 cubes	Builds bridge of 3 cubes. Imitates cross	Talks in sentences. Answers simple questions	Uses spoon well. Puts on shoes. Takes turns
2 years	Runs. Builds tower of 6 cubes	Builds tower of 6 cubes. Imitates circular stroke	Uses phrases. Understands simple directions	Verbalizes toilet needs. Plays with dolls
18 months	Walks without falling. Seats self. Tower of 3 cubes	Dumps pellet from bottle. Imitates crayon strokes	Jargons. Names pictures	Uses spoon with moderate spilling. Toilet regulated
12 months	Walks with help. Cruises. Prehends pellet with precision	Releases cube in cup	Says 2 or more words	Cooperates in dressing. Gives toy. Finger feeds
40 weeks	Sits alone. Creeps. Pulls to feet. Crude prehensory release	Combines two cubes	Says one word. Heeds his name	Plays simple nursery games. Feeds self cracker

28 weeks	Sits leaning forward on hands. Grasps cube. Rakes at pellet	Transfers cube from hand to hand	Crows. Vocalizes eagerness. Listens to own vocalizations	Plays with feet and toys. Expectant in feeding situations
16 weeks	Head steady. Symmetrical postures. Hands open	Competent eye following. Regards rattle in hand	Coos. Laughs. Vocalizes socially	Plays with hands and dress. Recognizes bottle. Poises mouth for food
4 weeks	Head sags. Tonic neck reflex. Hands fisted	Stares at surroundings. Restricted eye following	Small throaty sounds. Heeds bell	Regards faces

[a] A. Gesell & C. Amatruda. *Developmental Diagnosis.*

TABLE 3. Height and Weight Norms for American Children[a]

Boys			*Girls*	
Weight	*Height*	*Age*	*Weight*	*Height*
7.5 pounds	19.9 inches	Birth	7.4 pounds	19.8 inches
12.6	23.8	3 months	12.4	23.4
16.7	26.1	6 months	16.0	25.7
20.0	28.0	9 months	19.2	27.6
22.2	29.6	12 months	21.5	29.2
23.7	30.9	15 months	23.0	30.5
25.2	32.2	18 months	24.5	31.8
27.7	34.4	2 years	27.1	34.1
30.0	36.3	2½ years	29.6	36.0
32.2	37.9	3 years	31.8	37.7
34.3	39.3	3½ years	33.9	39.2
36.4	40.7	4 years	36.2	40.6
38.4	42.0	4½ years	38.5	42.0
40.5	42.8	5 years	40.5	42.9
45.6	45.0	5½ years	44.0	44.4
48.3	46.3	6 years	46.5	45.6

[a]Nelson, W. E., et al. *Textbook of Pediatrics,* Philadelphia: Saunders, 1969. Pp. 42–44.

The following are useful "signposts" for American children:

Weight

1. Average birth W, both sexes is 7 lb. 6 oz.
2. From 3-12 months W (lb.) – age in months plus 11.
3. At 30 months W = 30 lb.
4. At 3.5 years W = 35 lb.
5. At 4-8 years W (lb.) = 6 times age in years plus 12.
6. From 8-12 years W (lb.) = 6 times age in years plus 5.

Height

1. Average birth length, both sexes, is 20 in.
2. At 12 months H is 30 in.
3. From 2-14 years H (in.) = 2½ times age in years plus 30

(Weech, 1954)

TABLE 4. Inventory of Developmental Tasks Santa Clara, California, Unified School District

Developmental Ability Areas	*Age Levels*			
	Preschool	*5 – 5½ years*	*6 – 6½ years*	*7 years*
Motor Coordination	Creep Walk Run Jump Hop Balance on one foot	Skip Balance on walking beam	Demonstrate right and left Jump rope assisted	Jump rope alone
Visual Motor	Follow target with eyes String beads Copy circle Use scissors Copy cross	Copy square Tie shoes	Copy letters Copy sentences	Copy diamond
Visual Perception	Match color objects Match form objects Match size objects Match size and form on paper	Match numbers Match letters	Match direction on design Isolate visual images	Match words
Visual Memory	Recall of animal pictures	Recall of a 2-picture sequence	Recall of a 3-picture sequence	Recall of word forms

TABLE 4. Inventory of Developmental Tasks Santa Clara, California, Unified School District (cont'd)

Developmental Ability Areas	*Age Levels*			
	Preschool	*5 – 5½ years*	*6 – 6½ years*	*7 years*
Visual Memory (cont'd)	Name objects from memory Recall of a 3-color sequence	Reproduce design from memory	Recall of a 3-part design	
Auditory Perception	Discrimination between common sounds Identify common sounds	Locate source of sound Match beginning sounds	Hear fine differences between similar sounds Match rhyming sounds	Match ending sounds
Auditory Memory	Perform 3 commands	Repeat a sentence Repeat tapping sequence	Repeat 4 numbers Recall story facts	Repeat 5 numbers
Language		Give personal information Describe simple objects	Relate words and pictures Define words	Uses correct grammar
Conceptual		Assign number value	Identify positions Tell how two items are alike	Sort objects two ways

DISCUSSION

1. In the first part of the assignment involving observing a child at each of the different age levels, was the child's behavior more similar to that of the preceding or of the following age? That is, is a 4-year-old more like a 3-year-old or a 5-year-old? In what ways?
2. Also, in the first part of the assignment, what specific behaviors or characteristics best distinguished each age level?
3. How accurate were you in estimating the children's ages?
4. In each case, how confident were you of your estimate? Explain.
5. What aspects of behavior were more useful than others in providing you with clues?
6. In individual cases, were there any aspects of behavior that misled you? Describe.
7. Did you attempt to elicit any specific behaviors from the children? How were these helpful to you in assessing the age level?
8. What did you learn from this observation?

Observation 6

Specimen Record

The purpose of this observation is to follow the procedure employed by the psychological ecologists in order to gain firsthand information concerning the strengths and weaknesses of this approach.

Choose an elementary school age child. Follow him and observe his behavior for as many different time periods throughout the day as is feasible. To obtain a specimen record for a single child, the ecologists use approximately five observers rotating every 30 minutes, thus obtaining a running account over an extended period of time. Clearly, observation is a demanding task. Such an approach is impossible for this observation; consequently, sampling different time periods will yield information on the child's behavior in different behavior settings. If possible, this observation should cover two hours, perhaps broken up into half hour segments.

Describe briefly the behavior setting in which each of the observations occur and mark off the behavior episodes. Use the definitions and the examples provided in the discussion of psychological ecology.

Discuss the following questions:

1. What are some of the problems of the ecological approach as you experienced them?
2. Do you agree with the claim by the ecologists that only this approach captures the richness and complexity of human behavior?
3. To what extent do you feel that some of your personal biasses (assumptions about human behavior, prejudices, your own needs and feelings) affected your observations? How might one attempt to eliminate some of these biasses?
4. In what ways do you feel the particular behavior settings affected the child's behavior in those settings?
5. To what extent do you feel the child you observed is representative of children of his age level? In other words, to what extent are you able to generalize from this sample of one child to the entire age group?
6. What did you learn from this observation?

Observation 7

Behavior Settings

The purpose of this observation is to attempt to substantiate the assertion made by psychological ecologists that the very nature of a behavior setting dictates to some extent the kinds of behavior that will be exhibited in that setting. Further, as the ecologists have shown, the proportion of individuals of different age levels frequenting various behavior settings varies depending on a number of characteristics of the behavior setting. Although casual observation reveals that fewer children visit jewelry stores than ice cream parlors, there is too little documentation and too little knowledge about the possible long-range effects on the child of the time he spends in one behavior setting compared with another.

Choose two different behavior settings from the following list (or others that may occur to you): supermarket, laundromat, department store, well-baby clinic, doctor's office, hamburger drive-in, restaurant, toy store. This observation will involve the following:

1. Select two or three mothers at random in each setting. Insofar as possible, observe each during her stay in that

setting, recording her behavior and her language, if possible, in relation to her children. The focus, then, will be on the mother's behavior and her interaction with her children.

2. Station yourself at an appropriate entrance or exit to the behavior setting (e.g., check out counter at supermarket). Estimate the ages of the children and the number in each family group.

Discussion:

1. What were some of the differences and some of the similarities between the mothers' behaviors in the two situations?
2. What were some of the similarities and differences in the children's behavior in the two situations?
3. What aspects or requirements of the behavior setting produced some of these behavior differences?
4. Could you speculate about possible long-range effects on the child or on the relation between the child and the parent as a result of continued interaction in a particular behavior setting?
5. What did you learn from this observation?

Observation 8

APPROACH

The purpose of this observation is to sharpen observational acuity by alerting the observer to specific categories of behavior. A possible danger of longhand running accounts of behavior characteristic of the ecological method is that specific, important behaviors may not emerge from the somewhat overwhelming mass of data. Consequently, significant behaviors that typify an individual in his interaction with others may not be identified. For example, using only gross categories, is a parent or a teacher characteristically positive or negative in his behavior toward a child or toward a group of children? To answer this question, it is necessary to categorize his ongoing behavior.

While the entire coding system in the APPROACH method discussed in the text, consisting of some 74 categories, is too involved to be employed by a beginning student of child observation, two areas are of great importance in understanding the emotional relationship between a child and an adult: negative reinforcement and positive reinforcement. The following are the nine specific behaviors described by Caldwell in each of these two areas:

Negative Reinforcement. This area encompasses behaviors best described as disrupting the emitted behavior of another person or group.

30 Withholds sanction. Subject protests, denies, or challenges a statement made to him, or refuses to carry out a requested act.
31 Shows discomfort. By behavior or verbalizations, the subject evidences fatigue, tension, fear, or pain.
32 Expresses displeasure. Subject emits an expression of unhappiness.
33 Criticizes or derogates. Subject is critical, derogatory, accusatory, belligerent, or thoughtless.
34 Expresses hostility. Subject gives an extreme statement of dislike or disapproval.
35 Interferes or restricts. Subject physically interferes with actions of another person.
36 Resists or rejects. Subject reacts to preceived interference with resistance.
37 Threatens or frightens. Subject gesturally or verbally threatens another person with censure, loss of privilege, or punishment.
38 Assaults. Physical action which involves any assault by one person upon the corpus of another person or object.

Positive Reinforcement. Each of these predicates is essentially a counterpart of one on the previous decile. All the categories refer to behavior which supports the ongoing behavior of another person or expresses a state of satisfaction with the self.

40 Permits or sanctions. Subject authorizes some proposed behavior.
41 Expresses solicitude. Subject expresses concern for well-being or comfort or contentment of another person.
42 Expresses pleasure. Subject emits signs of positive affect expression.
43 Approves, encourages. Subject enhances the self-esteem of person to whom the response is directed.
44 Expresses affection. Subject gives physical or verbal indications of love and affection.
45 Facilitates. Subject provides physical help to another person.
46 Excuses. Subject emits a response which rationalizes or defends another person's behavior.

47 Bargains, promises. Subject makes some kind of desired reinforcement contingent upon a particular type of response emission.

48 Protects, defends. Subject takes anticipatory action to defend the person or rights of another individual or item.

(Caldwell *et al.*, 1969, pp. 84-85)

There are two parts to this assignment. First, the student should attempt to apply the above 18 categories to the specimen record obtained in Observation 6 that involved observing and recording the behavior of an elementary school age child. The categories listed above are for recording an adult's behavior toward children. Since a large part of the Observation 6 record may not involve interaction with an adult, score only those parts in which such interaction occurred, applying the categories to the adult's behavior toward the child.

For the second part of the assignment, make a 30-minute observation of an adult-child interaction using the 18 categories. Do not make a longhand specimen record, but use the 18 reinforcement categories to record the ongoing interaction. Again, the categories should be applied to the adult's behavior toward one child or toward a group (as in the classroom or on the playground).

For both parts of the assignment, sum the frequencies under the two areas separately.

DISCUSSION

1. Did the use of the specific categories reveal information that might not have been apparent from observation alone? Explain.
2. Which categories were used more than others? Might some have been eliminated without loss of meaning?
3. Did you note any particular child behavior that preceded or followed a particular adult response? In other words, what effect did the child's behavior have on the adult's behavior, and vice versa?
4. What did you learn from this observation about observational method and about adult-child interaction?

Observation 9

Time Sampling

This observational assignment involves two parts in order to obtain information regarding (1) the relative problems involved in the use of time sampling for different child behaviors, and (2) age differences in these behaviors.

Select two child behaviors for time sampling observation. While the following are only suggestions, the student must make sure that the behaviors chosen occur with sufficient frequency so that time sampling is appropriate: quarrels, cooperation, initiation of social contacts, affectional behavior, attention- or approval-seeking from an adult, aggression, anger outbursts, engaged in active play vs. physically inactive, dependency behavior.

The behavior must be defined unambiguously so that it can be clearly distinguished from other, similar-appearing behaviors. In the Moss and Robson study described in the text, the four infant states were defined quite precisely. To cite another example, Beller (1955) used the following behaviors to denote dependency: seeking help, seeking physical contact, seeking proximity, seeking attention, and seeking recognition. Further, a definition was given for each of these behaviors.

The time interval should be approximately 30 seconds to 1 minute. Mark off the sheet with the behavior or behaviors down the left side and the time intervals across the top. Using the dependency example on the next page.

Depending in part on the behavior under investigation, the children should probably be observed as a group although with frequently-appearing behaviors and with behavior exhibited by a child individually, the children should be observed in random rotation. A total observation time of 30 minutes should be adequate, with the frequency scores ranging from 0 to 60. Depending upon the time and setting of the observation, two 20-minute observations might provide a more adequate sampling of the behavior.

Select two different age levels (preschool and elementary school age) for observing the two behaviors separately in order to respond to the following questions:

1. Which of the two behaviors you selected could be observed most clearly? Was this due in part to your definitions?
2. How did the two age levels differ in terms of frequency scores for the two behaviors?
3. From your age comparisons, can you conclude that time sampling is more appropriate for some behaviors than for others depending upon the age level studied? Explain.
4. Do you feel that the time periods (of the day) and the settings you observed yielded a representative sampling of the children's behavior? How might the behaviors vary depending upon these two variables?
5. How do you feel about the general adequacy and meaningfulness of time sampling as an observational technique as compared with the ecological approach?
6. What did you learn from this observation, either with regard to observational methodology or with regard to child behavior?

Time: 10:00 a. m.
Activity: Outside free play
Age group: Kindergarten

Dependency Behaviors	*Time intervals*				
	1 minute	2 minutes	3 minutes	4 minutes	etc.
Seeking help					
Seeking physical contact					
Seeking proximity					
Seeking attention					

Observation 10

Event Sampling

Choose a relatively frequently-occurring event. The event may be selected from the list by Barker included in the text or the student may use any other event that seems to be of significance in the lives of children; for example, a study of "children greeting each other" may reveal important dynamics of child behavior. It is important that the event be a fairly discrete and identifiable unit of behavior.

As with the ecological method, describe in as much detail as possible the entire ongoing sequence of behavior from the beginning until the end of the event as you have carefully defined it.

Although it is possible to observe a single child in event sampling in order to attempt to understand his behavior in a variety of situations, for this Observation it would be appropriate to study a larger sample of children, perhaps five girls and five boys.

Attempt to define aspects of the behavior sequence that appear with some frequency in the event sampled. In other words, determine if it is possible to identify sub-units of the larger behavioral unit. If so, develop a relatively small number of categories for coding the event you selected for observation.

Discuss the following questions:

1. Was your selection of an event appropriate so that (a) it occurred with sufficient frequency so that you were able to observe a minimum of ten occurrences of it, and (b) it was a clearly identifiable event distinguishable from the context of behavior in which it occurred?
2. What categories were you able to develop in order to code the behavior sequence? Did any clear patterns emerge to help you understand some of the dynamics underlying the event or some of the correlates associated with the occurrence of the event? For example, in the study of discipline described in the text, Clifford found age, and the level of communication skills associated with age, to be an important factor in the frequency of disciplinary episodes and in the type of discipline employed by the parent.
3. What did your analysis of the event reveal about the personalities and behavioral adjustments of the individual children you observed? How did the children differ from one another in these areas?
4. What do you feel are some of the advantages and disadvantages of event sampling as an observational technique?
5. How does event sampling compare with unstructured psychological ecology and with time sampling in terms of how well they help the observer observe, record, and understand child behavior?
6. What did you learn about child behavior and about observational techniques from this observation?

Observation 11

Ratings

The purpose of this observation is to acquaint the student with the rating method for summarizing and quantifying observational impressions. The procedure to be followed will be similar to that employed by Cobb et al. (1967) in their attempt to determine the extent of agreement between observers in their ratings of the behavior of newborn infants.

In the Cobb study 114 healthy babies from one to three days of age were observed for 20 minutes in a fairly standardized situation. Subsequently, the observers rated the infants on six scales: activity level, attention span, persistence, alertness, irritability, and social responsiveness.

The standardized procedure was as follows:

> The selected infant was placed on four thicknesses of smooth blanket on his own crib table, with his head to the left of the observer who was handling him. Since most infants spontaneously roll to the right, the observers could see his face in this position. If he persistently rolled to the left during this initial period of the observation, his position was changed so that his head was at the opposite end of the table. Before the

beginning of the observation proper, a check was made to be sure that he met the criterion of being awake and the observation was continued only while he remained awake.

Observer 1, who rated all the infants, then bent over him and observed him for one minute. Next she moved about to see if he made an attempt to follow her with his eyes. She then bent over him again and spoke to him, noting whether he fixated upon her, changed facial expression, or changed his general bodily activity. Next she dangled a red embroidery hoop from a string approximately 12 inches from the infant's head and in his line of vision, to see if he fixated upon it. The hoop was then moved down in a horizontal arc to his right or left, depending upon the position in which he was lying, to see to what extent he followed it with his eyes (and sometimes with his head and body). This procedure was repeated at least twice, and more often if the infant's response was in doubt. The distance of the hoop from the infant's eyes was varied somewhat because not all infants fixate at the same point.

Then the observer shook a rattle and subsequently rang a bell approximately 12 inches from the infant's head and beyond his line of vision. The nature and strength of the response as well as the length of time the infant seemed to be reacting to sound were noted.

Next, if he was sucking his fingers they were removed from his mouth to see whether he would return to this activity; if he was not sucking his fingers, they were placed in his mouth, to see whether he accepted this change or withdrew them.

Observer 1 then picked him up and held him to her shoulder, with his head high enough so that the other observer(s) could see how he adjusted to this change in position. Then the infant was shifted to her arms, and she swayed gently and spoke to him in soft tones. This procedure was repeated at the end of the observation with one of the other observers handling the infant, to give each observer an equal opportunity to watch the infant's response to these shifts in position.

The infant was then placed on the side opposite to that to which he had rolled earlier, and it was observed whether he remained where placed or rolled back to his former position.

(pp. 255-256)

The six scales were defined in these terms:

> *Activity level* was rated on the basis of the proportion of the observation period during which the infant engaged in observable movements, segmental or involving the whole body, and the vigor, rapidity, and definiteness of the movements.
>
> *Attention span* was defined as the length of time the infant sustained a specific response to an identifiable stimulus; judgments were based on the length of time the infant fixated on, or followed with his eyes, an object or person, and to a lesser degree the length of time he attended to an auditory stimulus.
>
> *Persistence* was rated on the basis of the infant's response to having his fingers removed from or placed in his mouth, and his response to the imposed shifts in position; these responses were considered indications of the strength of his tendency to continue an ongoing activity or to resist change.
>
> *Alertness* was judged on the basis of the infant's apparent awareness of his surroundings, and his response to various specific stimulations, as demonstrated by changes in facial expression and in bodily activity. Examples are a startle reaction to the sound of the bell or a decrease in general bodily activity in response to a soft voice. (Duration of response was not taken into account in making this rating, as this aspect of infant behavior was included in the rating of attention span).
>
> *Irritability* was judged on the basis of the frequency, duration, and intensity of fussing/crying which did not appear to be related to identifiable physical discomfort, and which persisted despite efforts to quiet or distract the infant during the observation period.
>
> *Social responsiveness* was rated on the basis of the frequency, duration, and intensity of the infant's responses to the observers, depending on visual, auditory, and tactual stimulation, and demonstrated by a change in facial expression, bodily movements, and, occasionally, by vocalization.
>
> (page 257)

Each scale was 200 mm long. The observer could place his ratings anywhere along the line. "A numerical score was later given to each rating by dividing each scale of 200 millimeters into 20 units of 10 millimeters or one centimeter, and assigning the value of the nearest point to the rating. The possible range of ratings on each scale was, therefore, 0 to 20, with 20 representing the raters' conception of the highest degree, 10 the average, and 0 the least, of the behavioral characteristic rated."

For the present observation the student should observe at least five infants under six months of age. It would be well to observe the infants for two separate periods. In the first period, the student should familiarize himself with the six scales and their definitions and should identify some of the behaviors on which his observational ratings will be based. In addition, the student should compare the infants to be rated on the six behavioral scales, since nearly all such ratings are *relative* in nature (unlike such *absolute* physical scales as height, weight, and temperature).

Although the student should attempt to standardize the second observational situation to some extent, he should not attempt as rigorous an approach as that employed in the Cobb study. Following this second observation, the student should rate each of the infants on the six scales, rating all of the infants on one dimension before going on to the next scale. Since research has found that it is not feasible in terms of accuracy and reliability to make distinctions finer than that required by a seven- to nine-point scale, seven-point scales should be used, with 7 representing the highest degree, 4 average, and 1 the least of that characteristic. For example:

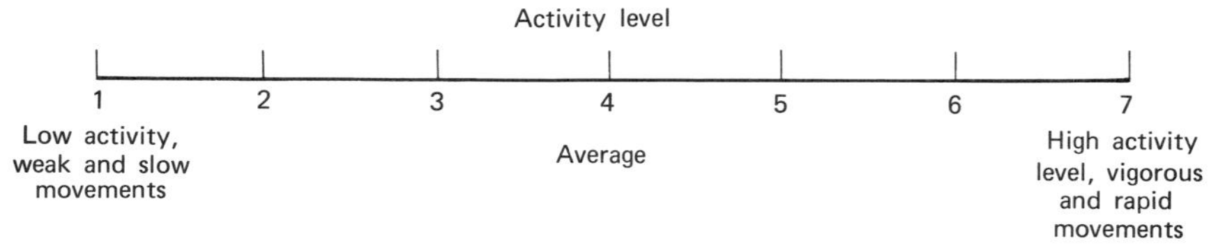

For each rating, the student should write a brief description of the observational evidence on which the rating is based. Ratings are meaningful only to the extent that the rater can justify the basis for them, citing specific behaviors.

If possible, it would be valuable to obtain ratings on the infants by two students, with a comparison of areas of agreement and disagreement and a discussion to determine the reasons for any discrepancies.

DISCUSSION

1. If you were to judge the certainty with which you made your ratings on a seven-point scale from seven-Very Certain to one-Uncertain, how would you rate your ratings on the five infants? In other words, do you feel your ratings were based on an adequate sample of behavior?
2. Did you find that some dimensions were easier to rate than others? Why? Did some require more extensive observations than others? Which ones?
3. What were some of the differences among the infants that became readily apparent from your observations?
4. How did the rating scales guide your observations in alerting you to specific aspects of behavior.
5. To what use might ratings of this kind be put? How might they be useful?
6. What did you learn from this observation?

Observation 12

Miniature Situations

This observation will be largely methodological in nature in that comparisons will be made between various miniature situations in terms of their effectiveness in revealing psychologically meaningful information about the child. The appropriateness of a situation for different age levels will also be examined.

As we have seen from the discussion in the text, most studies using miniature situations have been designed to investigate a specific behavior: honesty, fears, aggression, and maternal teaching style. The Santostefano research, on the other hand, appears to examine the general area of parent-child relations, attempting to elicit a wide variety of behaviors. Moreover, some of the research has employed ratings or check lists in order to quantify the observational data, while in other research general clinical evaluations of the individuals are made.

For the present observation the student should select approximately three situations using several children at two different age levels, preschool and elementary school age. The following are suggestions only; the student should feel free to devise other situations: child talking on telephone (pretending that he is talking to a friend or that he is his mother talking to someone); child pretending to be a teacher or a mother reading a book to a young child; child putting a difficult jigsaw puzzle together; child feeding a doll.

The student may draw up a small number of categories for recording the behavior, or a longhand account of the child's behavior can be made, with an attempt later to quantify the material into meaningful themes or categories.

DISCUSSION

1. How successful were the miniature situations you selected in eliciting significant psychological information?
2. What age differences did you note in terms of (a) behavior exhibited, and (b) the appropriateness of the miniature situations you used?
3. What categories or themes did you use in rating or recording the behavior?
4. What other situations do you think might be employed to uncover meaningful psychological data?
5. Did you ask the children questions during the miniature situation? How important do you feel it is to combine miniature situations with interviewing as Santostefano has done?
6. What did you learn about observational methods and about children from this observation?

Observation 13

Questionnaires and Inventories

The inventories developed to assess various personality characteristics in older children have been, for the most part, carefully standardized, with norms available so that a given child's score can be interpreted by comparing it with the norms for his age and sex group. Though perhaps less well standardized, questionnaires administered to younger children frequently reveal a great deal about the child's thought processes. This is particularly instructive at a time when the child's thinking is undergoing marked and relatively rapid change.

The present observation will involve administering a series of general information items to a small number of children. These items were drawn from the early work by Probst (1931), and have been used in several subsequent studies (Medinnus, 1959; Templin, 1958).

Since these items were designed originally for young children, the student should select approximately five children between the ages of four and six years. The questions must be administered individually with the child's answers recorded by the observer.

INFORMATION QUESTIONNAIRE

1. What state do we live in?
2. What is the name of the county we live in?
3. What is the largest city in (name of state)?
4. How many pennies in a nickel?
5. How many eggs in a dozen?
6. Friday, Saturday, Sunday—What day comes after Sunday?
7. What time or what o'clock is it at noon?
8. Who was the first President of the United States?
9. What are the colors of the flag?
10. What is a helicopter?
11. What shape is the sun?
12. What is snow made of?
13. What makes it light in the daytime?
14. What colors are the keys on a piano?
15. Whom was Red Riding Hood going to see?
16. What did Cinderella lose at the ball?
17. How do you play a saxophone?
18. When the three bears came home, whom did they find in bed?
19. What was the name of the boy who climbed the beanstalk?
20. What are little chickens hatched from?
21. What do bees make that we eat?
22. A baby dog is called a puppy; what is a baby cow called?
23. What do we call a butterfly before it becomes a butterfly?
24. Where does wool come from?
25. What color is an apple before it is ripe?
26. What is the outside of a tree called?
27. Who makes money by cutting hair?
28. What does a carpenter do?
29. To whose office do we go to get a tooth pulled?
30. What is butter made from?
31. What animal do we get bacon from?
32. What is the outside of an egg called?
33. What do we use to put a screw into wood?
34. What is the brake on a car for?
35. What is a thermometer for?

36. What makes a sailboat go?
37. In what game do you have a touchdown?
38. In what game do you have a homerun?
39. You know how to play "The Farmer in the Dell." Who does the farmer choose?
40. What people lived in America before the white man did?

DISCUSSION

1. What were some of the areas of accuracy or inaccuracy in the children's responses? That is, could you categorize their correct and incorrect responses in such a way that would help to explain reasons for their knowledge (or lack of it)? For example, one might expect that children's information would be incorrect on topics outside their range of experience or in areas beyond their ability to comprehend.
2. What did the children's answers tell you about their backgrounds, or about the environment in which they are being reared?
3. What were some of the questions that surprised you as far as the children's accuracy or inaccuracy in responding?
4. What were some of the random comments made by the children that revealed something about their thought processes?
5. What were some of your general observational impressions of the different children during the testing situation? That is, did you receive impressions with regard to characteristics other than the amount of information the children possessed, such as intellectual level, alertness, curiosity, impulsiveness, self-confidence, verbal ability, and ability to relate to an adult?
6. What are some of the things that a questionnaire tells us about a child that perhaps could not be learned through observation of his behavior?
7. What did you learn about the questionnaire method and about children from this observation?

Observation 14

Personality Appraisal Techniques and Psychometric Tests of Ability

In this observation the student has a choice between one dealing with personality appraisal and one concerning intellectual functioning.

Personality Appraisal

Select two children of approximately the same age in the eight to ten year age range.

Use the picture provided in Figure 2, and perhaps several others of a somewhat ambiguous nature drawn from a magazine or a children's book. These might depict a child and an adult in order to elicit information concerning the child's relationship with adults. They might explore the use of a picture showing several children, perhaps in a controversial situation, in an attempt to elicit the child's feelings regarding peer group interaction.

Ask the children to tell a story about the picture, describing what led up to the scene depicted, what is occurring, and what the outcome will be. Encourage them to tell how the characters feel and what they are saying. Record their stories.

Examine the stories for possible themes or significant qualities. As in the Alexander Picture Story scoring system, attempt to evaluate the stories on two global dimensions: positiveness or negativeness of emotional expression and whether the characters are viewed in a hostile or friendly fashion.

To the same two children administer the sentence completion test described on pages 45 and 46. Again, score their responses on the same two general dimensions as their stories and for other themes that seem to emerge. List the bases for your evaluations.

Attempt to draw together the data from the two techniques used for each child and write an interpretive description of some of the personality dynamics that you feel are operating.

DISCUSSION

1. How certain do you feel about your interpretations of the information provided by the two children on the picture story and sentence completion measures?
2. What other observations would you like to make on the children in order to add to your knowledge about them? And what other kinds of information would you like to have in order to better understand these two children?
3. What behaviors, mannerisms, or personality indications did you observe about the children in the test situations?
4. What did you learn about personality appraisal techniques and about children from this observation?

Measures of Intellectual Ability

Psychometric tests of ability are carefully standardized in terms of order of presentation of the items and of the manner in which they are presented. Further, an IQ score cannot be computed unless the instructions concerning the number of items and which specific items to be administered are followed carefully. Consequently, it would be impossible for a student without extensive training in psychological testing to properly administer a psychometric test. However, a number of different measures have been developed for estimating a child's ability. For example, vocabulary, since it is a reflection of abstract ability, is a strong indicator of intelligence. Also, there is good evidence that tests of memory span assess basic intellectual potential. A third method involves scoring children's drawings of a human figure. The Goodenough Draw-A-Man Test was one of the earliest group tests of intelligence (Goodenough, 1926). In this test the child is asked to draw "the best man he can." The scoring is based on the number of details included in the drawing. The test is relatively easy to administer and score. However, the scores correlate only moderately with other more sophisticated measures of intelligence and with school achievement. The Draw-A-Man test does provide a useful gross estimate of the child's intellectual ability level.

For this observation, select approximately five children at each of two age levels: four and six years. The test can be administered to each child individually, though it was developed for group administration. Provide each child with a pencil and 8½ x 11 inch sheet of paper. Follow these verbal instructions fairly closely: "I would like to have you draw a picture of a man. Draw the very best picture you can. Go ahead and begin." Do not offer any hints or suggestions although you may encourage the child by saying, "That's right, draw the best man you can." Following the completion of the drawing, be sure to praise the children for their effort.

Rather than presenting the entire scoring system here, only those points which are typically found at the two age levels will be listed. Score one point for each item listed in the drawing.

1. Head present
2. Legs present
3. Arms present (these may be attached to the head)
4. Trunk present (this may be a straight line)
5. Length of trunk greater than breadth
6. Attachment of arms and legs (both must be attached to the trunk)
7. Neck present (must be distinct from head and trunk)
8. Eyes present
9. Nose present
10. Mouth present
11. Nostrils shown
12. Hair shown

13. Clothing present (any indication of clothing; single dot or circle placed near center of trunk is usually intended as a navel)
14. Fingers present
15. Correct number of fingers shown
16. Proportion. Head. (area of the head not more than one half or less than one tenth that of the trunk; score rather leniently)
17. Motor Coordination. Lines A (all lines reasonably firm, for the most part meeting each other cleanly at points of junction, without marked tendency to cross or overlap, or to leave gaps between the ends)
18. Ears present
19. Eye detail. Brow or lashes or both shown
20. Eye detail. Pupil shown (if only dot is shown for eye, this point may not be credited)

The number of points to be expected of an average child at the two age levels are: four points at age four and twelve points at age six. In the Draw-A-Man test, the number of points included in the drawing is converted to Mental Age, this formular is used:

$$IQ = \frac{\text{Mental Age}}{\text{Chronological Age}} \times 100$$

Thus, a four-year-old with a Mental Age of four would have an IQ of 100.

DISCUSSION

1. What were some of the behaviors you noted while the children were making their drawings? Did these furnish any clues to personality, such as self-confidence, motivation, need for adult approval?
2. To what extent do you think motor coordination or artistic ability affected the drawings?
3. In what ways might the child's background experiences have affected the quality of his drawing?
4. What did you learn about children's performance and about this method of assessment from this observation?

Observation 15

Interview

Interviews may be structured, with a specific set of questions to be asked or they may be unstructured and open-ended; they may be designed as a clinical tool to understand an individual case or they may be used to obtain information concerning certain research problems such as the relation between mothers' attitudes toward aggression and dependency and their children's nursery school behavior; finally, they may cover broad areas of parent behavior and attitudes and of family interaction or they may focus on narrow, carefully defined topics related to childrearing such as toilet training.

Whatever the purpose of the interview—whether to elicit concerning such sensitive topics as marital compatibility or more objective information pertaining to an individual's attitude toward the current political situation—it is extremely important to set at ease the interviewee, to establish initial rapport with him so that he will talk freely with a minimum of defensiveness and anxiety. Mutual trust and respect between the interviewer and interviewee are essential. Also, the manner in which the interview is begun and ended is extremely important. In the present interview, the student might indicate to the mother that he is trying to learn about parents and children, and the best way to do this is to ask an expert, namely, a mother. At the end of the interview, thank the mother for her cooperation and assure her that she has been most helpful to you.

For this observation, the student should focus on the principal variables describing the psychological atmosphere of the home: acceptance-rejection and autocratic-democratic. An interview schedule designed to elicit information pertaining to these two areas should be constructed. Four mothers should be interviewed: mothers of a preschool boy and girl, and mothers of a school age (third through sixth grade) boy and girl.

If possible, tape record the interviews; otherwise, take some handwritten notes during the interview in as unobtrusive a manner as possible.

Following the interviews (not necessarily immediately following) rate the mother on the two major variables, using the Fels ratings scales on pages 52 and 53.

The following are offered merely as suggestions of the type of questions that might be included in your interview schedule:

1. Describe a typical weekday for your child. And a typical Saturday.
2. Describe your child as you see him. Is he fairly good natured, fairly easy to get along with? Easy or difficult to control?
3. Is C. in good health? Has he been ill very much in the past? Is he about as healthy as most children his age?
4. Does C. get hurt easily? How does he act when he gets hurt?
5. Does C. require quite a bit of extra attention when ill or hurt? How do you feel about this?
6. What would you say and how would you feel if someone, say a neighbor, criticized your C. while talking to you?
7. Can C. take care of himself in the group he plays with? With brothers and sisters? Or does he usually get the

worst end of it? Do you sometimes have to step in and help out?

8. Do you feel that children usually should be held responsible for their behavior? By that I mean if a child does something he shouldn't, should he be excused on the grounds that he is too little or too young to know what he should and should not do? How old do children have to be before you think they are capable of knowing what is right and what is wrong? When should they be held accountable for what they do?
9. When C. is out playing, do you know where he is most of the time? Do you know what he is doing? Do you tend to worry when you don't know where he is? Do you worry about whether C. is getting into trouble, or into dangerous situations, etc., when he is not where you can watch him?
10. What do you think about the idea some parents have of deliberately exposing their children to tough situations on the grounds that this is good for them? Don't you think that it's good for children to have a few hard knocks in order to prepare them for adult life?
11. Some parents seem to let the children run the house. What do you think about this? Should parents give in to the child's wishes and whims? To what extent?
12. Do you try to teach C. to take care of himself in many ways—or do you try to help him quite a bit? Don't you think that children can get hurt and get into trouble if they are allowed too much freedom and if they are "on their own" too much? In general, to what degree should children be allowed to be their own boss? What are some of the things children should be allowed to decide for themselves?
13. Should parents try to make their children's lives easier in various ways than they had it?
14. What are some of the rules and regulations you have laid down that you feel C. should abide by? What are some of the things he is not allowed to do?
15. What are some of the things, such as responsibilities,

behavior, etc., that you expect of C? Does he have any regular chores?

16. Is C. fairly obedient? Does he usually do what he is told without putting up a big fuss or fight? Can you usually get him to do what you want?
17. How do you feel when C. contradicts something you tell him to do—or puts off doing it? Should parents tolerate this? Why? Why not? Are there any exceptions? What do you usually do when C. refuses to do something you tell him to do? How do you feel?
18. How do you feel when C. argues with a command or a request you have given him?
19. Is it wise for parents to give in to their children? Explain.
20. How far should parents go in allowing children to question the discipline used? To what extent, and in what situations, if any, should children be given some choice as far as whether or not to do what the parent suggests or requests?
21. Can children always be given reasons for rules and regulations and punishments?
22. What are some of the things C. does that require punishment? How do you usually punish C.? How does he react to this?
23. Do you consider yourself quite strict or rather lenient? Explain.
24. How worried should parents be about losing their children's affection as a result of punishing them?
25. Should parents ever ignore their children's misbehavior? If so, when? Why shouldn't they ignore misbehavior?
26. All children can get pretty annoying at times. What are some of the things C. does that irritate you, that get on your nerves? Does he make you pretty nervous at times? How?
27. How do you think other people see C, such as relatives, neighbors, teacher?
28. Who would you say C. takes after? In what ways is he like you? not like you?

DISCUSSION

1. What were some of the differences you noted on the two dimension depending upon the age and sex of the child?
2. To what extent do you think you can generalize from your small sample with regard to the issues of child-rearing you explored? In other words, how representative was your sample?
3. On what did you base your ratings? Which specific answers did you consider in making your ratings?
4. How successful were you in eliciting informating concerning the two dimensions? What other questions might you have asked?
5. What were some aspects of childrearing other than the two major variables that you noted from the interviews?
6. What were some of the personality characteristics which the mothers revealed during the interviews—for example, anxiety, need for approval, self-confidence, unhappiness.
7. How do you think the psychological atmosphere of a specific home affects that child's personality development?
8. What did you learn about interviewing as a method and about mothers' childrearing attitudes and practices from this observation?

Part II

Topical Research Projects

Observation 16

Motor Development

Since early motor development follows a clear sequential pattern, it is possible to determine a child's developmental level by observing his behavior on a variety of motor tasks. While little information is available concerning the long range impact on adult personality of motor capabilities in the childhood years, motor proficiency is a valued trait for boys throughout the childhood years and thus it is likely to affect his self-concept.

In recent years, a tremendous amount of attention has been paid to deviations in early motor development, particularly fine motor coordination. Such deviations are seen as indicators of minimal brain damage that, in turn, is thought to produce learning disability in the early school years. A number of curriculum-type programs have been developed (e.g., Frostig, Kephart, Winterhaven) to train children in the motor coordination and perceptual areas.

PURPOSE

The purpose of this observation is to focus the student's attention on differences among children at a given age level in their motor coordination as well as on differences between age levels in this area.

SUBJECTS

Select two girls and two boys at two age levels, three and five years.

PROCEDURE

Administer the following motor development items to the children individually. Use the work sheets provided for the copying items.

Gross motor items

1. Walk – child walks forward and backward for a distance of approximately 20 feet in a smooth cross-pattern movement.
2. Run – child runs and stops on signal from observer.
3. Jump with feet together – child stands with both feet together and jumps forward as far as possible.
4. Hop – child hops on one foot approximately ten feet, then turns and hops back using alternate foot.
5. Balance on one foot – child balances on one foot for five seconds, repeat with other foot.
6. Skip – child is to skip approximately 20 feet alternating feet.
7. Catching a ball (medium-size rubber ball)
8. Throwing a ball (medium-size rubber ball)

Fine motor coordination

1. Copy a circle – for copying items have child make two attempts.
2. Use scissors – draw a straight line on a sheet of paper for child to cut.
3. Copy a cross
4. Copy a square
5. Tie shoes
6. Draw a house

7. Copy letters and numbers
8. Copy triangle

Observe the child carefully while he is attempting to perform each item. Note his approach to the task and specific aspects of body and limb movements. For both gross motor and fine motor items, note first whether the child is able to perform the task. Second, for the gross motor items rate the child's performance on a five-point scale from 1–poor coordination, awkward to 5–well coordinated, agile. On the fine motor items rate performance on a five-point scale from 1–poor control, clumsy to 5–good control, dextrous.

RESULTS AND DISCUSSION

1. What age differences in motor coordination became apparent from your observations?
2. Were there sex differences with regard to gross versus fine motor coordination? Were there any sex differences on specific items?
3. Did you observe any relations among the tasks–that is, was a child who did well on one task also able to do well on the others?
4. What personality characteristics were revealed by the children's approach to and performance on these motor tasks–for example, self-confidence, self-consciousness, dependency? Were there differences, in this respect, between the fine and gross motor items?
5. To what extent do you think practice affects the child's motor functioning?
6. What did you learn about motor development from this observation?

SELECTED BIBLIOGRAPHY

Bayley, N. Comparison of mental and motor test scores for ages 1-15 months by sex, birth order, race, geographical location, and education of parents. *Child Development,* 1965, **36**, 379–411.

Cratty, B. *Perceptual and motor development in infants and children.* New York: Macmillan, 1970.

Espenschade, A. S., & Eckert, H. M. *Motor development.* Columbus, Ohio: Merrill, 1967.

Frostig, M., & Horn, D. *The Frostig program for the development of visual perception.* Chicago: Follett, 1964.

Frostig, M., Maslow, P., Lefever, D., & Whittlesey, J. The Marianne Frostig Developmental Test of Visual Perception. Palo Alto: Consulting Psychologists Press, 1964.

Gesell, A., & Amatruda, C. *Developmental diagnosis: Normal and abnormal child development.* New York: Hoeber, 1941.

Gesell, A., Halverson, H., Thompson, H., Ilg, F., Castner, B., Ames, L., & Amatruda, C. *The first five years of life.* New York: Harper & Row, 1940.

Kephart, N. C. *The slow learner in the classroom.* Columbus, Ohio: Merrill, 1960.

McGraw, M. B. *Growth: A study of Johnny and Jimmy.* New York: Appleton-Century, 1935.

Sloan, W. Lincoln-Oseretsky Motor Development Scale. *Genetic Psychology Monographs,* 1955, **51**, 183-252.

Sutphin, F. *A perceptual testing-training handbook for first grade teachers.* Winter Haven Lions Research Foundations Inc., 1964.

Watson, E. H., & Lowrey, G. H. *Growth and development of children.* Chicago: Yearbook Publishers, 1958.

Wellman, B. L. Motor achievements of preschool children. *Child Education,* 1937, **13**, 311-316.

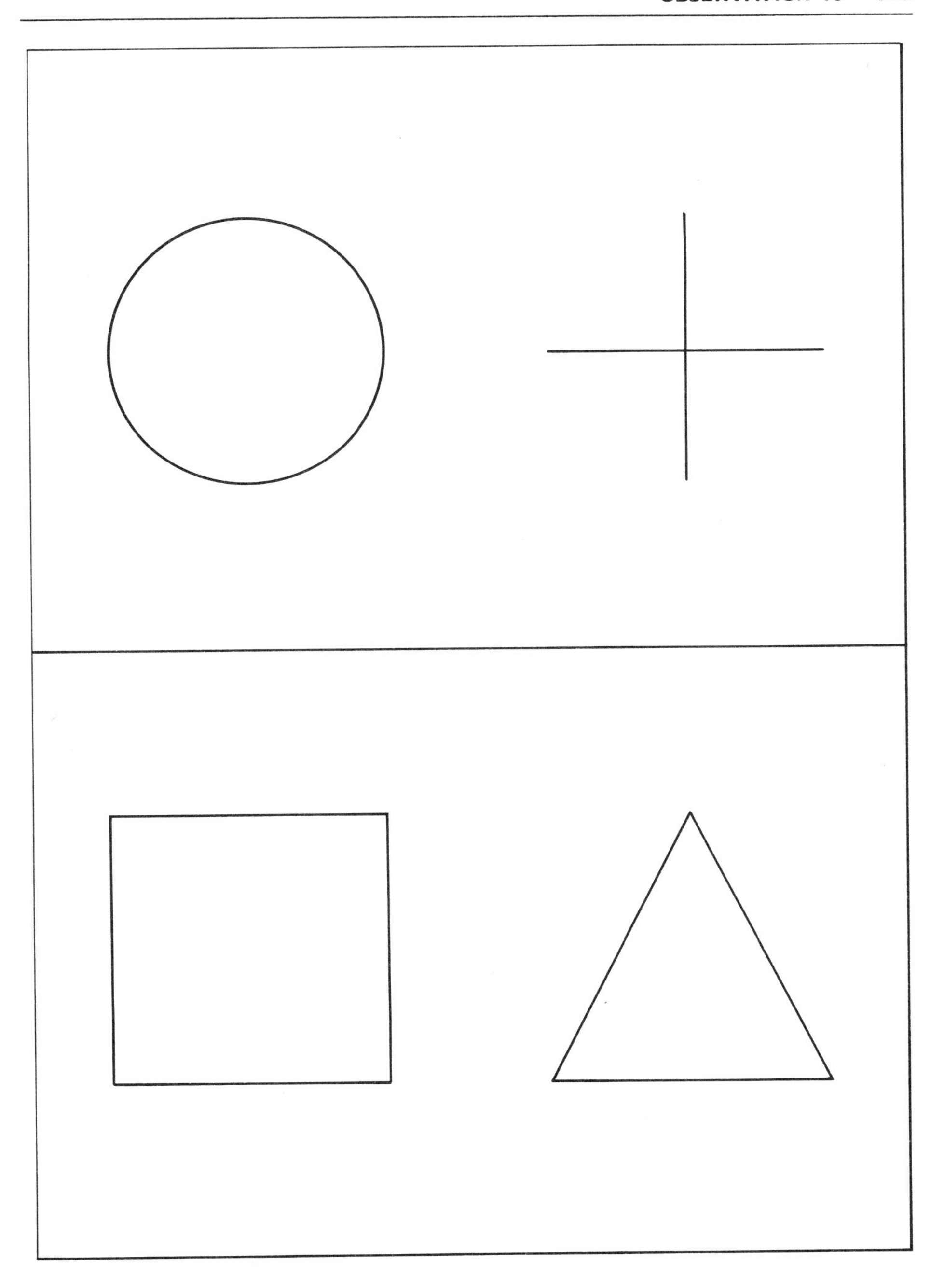

ABESK

nbefj

Observation 17

Body Build: Identification and Preferences

There is a long history of interest in identifying the relation between body build and personality. The early work in this area was primarily speculative in nature, with many broad generalizations regarding differences in behavior associated with various physiques. More recently, a number of studies have been conducted using subjects from preschool through college age. These investigations have sought to determine (1) the relation between body build and various personality characteristics in children, and, (2) preferences among children for three main body types and the accuracy of self-identification in body build.

An example of the first approach was an extensive study by Walker (1962) in which 125 preschool children were rated by their teachers on 64 behavior items. The somatotyping used Sheldon's classification system that divides physiques into three main body types: endomorph, mesomorph, and ectomorph. With regard to the relations between the behavioral and physique data, many more of the predictions were confirmed for boys than for girls, suggesting that physical factors are more important in affecting the behavior of boys. The mesomorphic body build showed the strongest relationship to the behavioral ratings, especially for boys.

> Characteristic of both boys and girls high in mesomorphy is a dominating assertiveness (leader in play, competitive, self-assertive, easily angered, attacks others, etc.), high energy output, openness of expression, and fearlessness. The girls combine the assertiveness with socialness, cheerfulness, and warmth. The boys' items give more suggestion of hostility (quarrelsome, revengeful, inconsiderate) and of an impulsive, headlong quality to their activity (daring, noisy, quick, accident prone, self-confident, etc.)
>
> (Walker, 1962, p. 78)

Some relationships were evident for the ectomorphic physique:

> In common for both sexes are items suggesting a certain aloofness. ... For boys, the items in general define a cautious, quiet child, not self-assertive, hesitant to give offense, looking to adults rather than to children for approval, sensitive, slow to recover from upsets. He appears lacking in energy reserves. ... For girls, the composite picture is similar but tends more to indicate a somberness of outlook—unfriendly, tense, not gay or cheerful, irritable.
>
> (p. 78)

In a related study, Walker (1963) asked the children's mothers to rate them on 68 descriptive adjectives and phrases. Some of the following physique-behavior relationships were found: endomorphic girl—cooperative, cheerful, low in tenseness and anxiety, and socially extravert; mesomorphic girl—energetic; mesomorphic boy—energetic, cheerful, and social; ectomorphic girl—uncooperative, not cheerful, anxious, and aloof; ectomorphic boy—unsocial, cooperative, and unaggressive.

With regard to accuracy of identification of one's own physique, Gellert, Girgus and Cohen (1970) presented children, ranging in age from 5 through 12 years, with photographs of children, with their own photograph included among the choices. The children were asked to find the photograph of themselves (the heads were covered) and to give reasons for their choice. The children were also shown photographs representing seven different body builds and were asked to choose the one that looked most like themselves. The results indicated that at all age levels the children performed better than chance in identifying their own photographs although accuracy of self-recognition increased with age.

Children hold clear stereotypes of the kinds of behavior expected from people differing in body build. This fact has been established by a number of studies in which children have been asked to assign various behavioral and personality characteristics to photographs or line drawings of individuals representing the mesomorphic, endomorphic, and ectomorphic body types. Moreover, these stereotypes are established as early as six years of age. In general, socially positive traits are assigned to mesomorphs while negative characteristics are associated with the ectomorph and endomorph. Moreover, physical attractiveness, however this is appraised by peers, is related to social acceptance (Kleck, Richardson, & Ronald, 1974). Furthermore, such overt physical characteristics as obesity and physical disability are associated with relatively low levels of social acceptance across a fairly broad age range.

PURPOSE

The purpose of this observation is to obtain information from children regarding their awareness of body build, their preference for body build, and the accuracy of their self-identification of body build.

SUBJECTS

Choose two boys and two girls at the following three age levels: 5, 7, and 9 years.

PROCEDURE

Using the accompanying sheet of body build silhouettes, ask the children individually the following questions:

1. Find the one that looks most like you. What makes you think that this one looks like you?
2. Which one would you most like to look like? Why would you like to look like that one?
3. Point to the one that looks like your best friend. What makes you think so?

4. Which child do you think:
   (a) can run the fastest? Why?
   (b) does the best school work? Why?
   (c) has the most friends? Why?
   (d) eats the most? Why?
   (e) is sick the most? Why?

RESULTS

1. Based on your own judgment of the children's body build, how accurate were they in self-identification? What words or what characteristics did the children use to describe their own physiques?
2. Was there agreement among the children in their preference for body build? Were there any age of sex differences? What reasons did the children give for their preferences?
3. Did the children tend to have friends whose body builds were the same as their own?
4. Did you note any pattern or consistency in the children's tendency to associate the six behavioral items with a particular body build?

DISCUSSION

1. To what extent do you think physique is important to children? At what age is body build most important to children? How early do stereotypes about body build and personality develop?
2. What age differences did you note in ability to verbalize reasons for choices?
3. What are some things that might be done to counteract negative self-feelings about body build?
4. What did you learn from this observation?

Extreme ectomorphy Mesomorphy Extreme endomorphy

SELECTED BIBLIOGRAPHY

Cabot, P. S. The relationship between characteristics of personality and physique in adolescents. *Genetic Psychology Monographs,* 1938, **20,** 3-120.

Cortes, J. B., & Gatti, F. M. Physique and self-description of temperament. *Journal of Consulting Psychology,* 1965, **29,** 432-439.

Davidson, M. A., McInnes, R. G., & Parnell, R. W. The distribution of personality traits in seven-year-old children: A combined psychological, psychiatric and somatotype study. *British Journal of Educational Psychology,* 1957, **27,** 48-61.

Dion, K., Berscheid, E., & Walster, E. What is beautiful is good. *Journal of Personality and Social Psychology,* 1972, **24,** 285-290.

Fisher, S., & Cleveland, S. E. *Body image and personality.* New York: Van Nostrand, 1958.

Gellert, E., Girgus, J., & Cohen, J. Children's awareness of their bodily appearance: A developmental study of factors associated with the body percept. *Genetic Psychology Monographs,* 1971, **84,** 109-174.

Hanley, C. Physique and reputation of junior high school boys. *Child Development,* 1951, **22,** 247-260.

Kleck, R., Richardson, S., & Ronald, L. Physical appearance cues and interpersonal attraction in children. *Child Development,* 1974, **45,** 305-310.

Lerner, R. M. Some female stereotypes of male body build-behavior relations. *Child Development,* 1969, **40,** 137-141.

Lerner, R. M., & Gellert, E. Body build identification, preference, and aversion in children. *Developmental Psychology,* 1969, **1,** 456-462.

Staffieri, J. R. A study of social stereotype of body image in children. *Journal of Personality and Social Psychology,* 1967, **7,** 101-104.

Walker, R. N. Body build and behavior in young children: I. Body build and nursery school teachers' ratings. *Monographs of the Society for Research in Child Development,* 1962, **27,** (Whole No. 84).

Walker, R. N. Body build and behavior in young children: II. Body build and parents' ratings. *Child Development,* 1963, **34,** 1-23.

Observation 18

Language Development

The development of language and communication in the child has attracted the attention of professional workers as well as parents for a very long time. Concern has been shown for normal development as well as for deviant development, such as delayed speech, misarticulations, stuttering, and organically related speech problems.

In the early baby biographies, described at the beginning of this manual, attempts were made to assess the extent and the growth of a child's vocabulary by recording all of his utterances and tabulating the number of different words used. Later investigators (e.g., McCarthy, 1930; Templin, 1957), using somewhat more controlled methods, explored some of the following aspects of language development: vocabulary, sentence length, rate and amount of speech, parts of speech, and age, sex, and social class differences. Other work in the area of language development has examined the role of language in communication and the function of language in the child's relationship with others. More recently, psycholinguists have focused on the development of the rules of grammar. For example, at what age is the child able to state the correct plural of a noun (e.g., dish–dishes, chair–chairs) and the correct past tense of a verb (e.g., jump–jumped, send–sent)? Concern with syntax has led psycholinguists to examine the growth toward adult usage with regard to sentence structure.

Brown and Berko (1960) have noted differences between children and adults in their word associations. In word association tests, adults typically respond with a word which is the same part of speech as the stimulus word while children give responses that, though related to the stimulus word, are based on aspects other than a grammatical one. For example, in response to the transitive verb "to send", children are likely to say, "letter" or "away" or "mail" while adults will give another transitive verb, such as "to deliver," "to receive," or "to mail." These investigators argue that this change with age in word association responses is a reflection of the child's gradual awareness of English syntax.

PURPOSE

The purpose of this observation is to examine children's word associations according to part of speech at two different age levels.

SUBJECTS

Select approximately five children from two age levels: five-six years and nine-ten years.

PROCEDURE

Following the procedure employed by Brown and Berko, administer individually the following word association test consisting of 36 stimulus words representing six parts of speech:

Count Nouns:	table, house, foot, needle, apple, doctor
Mass Nouns:	milk, water, sand, sugar, air, cheese
Adjectives:	dark, soft, cold, white, sweet, hard
Transitive Verbs:	to send, to bring, to find, to take, to hit, to invite
Intransitive Verbs:	to skate, to come, to live, to laugh, to stand, to walk
Adverbs:	quickly, slowly, sadly, now, softly, gently

Present the test in this manner: "This is a game called "say a word." Have you ever played "say a word"? Well, this is the way it works. I'm going to say a word and I want you to listen to my word and then say another word, not my word but a different word. Any word is all right so long as it's the first word that comes into your head when you hear my word. Are you ready?" Record the responses.

RESULTS

Score the responses according to whether or not the response word is of the same part of speech as the stimulus word.

DISCUSSION

1. Were there clear age differences in the number (or per cent) of homogeneous (same part of speech) responses?
2. Were there differences depending on the part of speech of the stimulus word? According to the Brown and Berko theory, what do these differences indicate with regard to the differential development of the awareness of various parts of speech?
3. What other aspects of the child's speech did you note, such as rate, correctness of pronunciation, vocabulary, and general language maturity? Did these impressions agree with the child's word association responses with regard to homogeneous parts of speech?
4. What did you learn about children's language development from this observation?

SELECTED BIBLIOGRAPHY

Berko, J., & Brown, R. Psycholinguistic research methods. In P. Mussen (Ed.), *Handbook of research methods in child development.* New York: Wiley, 1960. Pp. 517-557.

Brown, R., & Berko, J. Word association and the acquisition of grammar. *Child development,* 1960, **31**, 1-14.

Entwisle, D. R. *The word associations of young children.* Baltimore: John Hopkins, 1966.

Ervin, S., & Miller, W. Language development. In H. Stevenson (Ed)., *Child psychology, 62nd Yearbook of the National Society for the Study of Education.* Chicago: University of Chicago Press, 1963. Pp. 108-143.

McCarthy, D. Language development of the preschool child. *Institute of Child Welfare Monograph Series No. 4.* Minneapolis: University of Minnesota Press, 1930.

Templin, M. C. *Certain language skills in children.* Minneapolis: University of Minnesota Press, 1957.

Observation 19

Explanations of Physical Causality

It is readily apparent that children's thinking differs from that of adults. The young child has a limited range of knowledge and experience, and this affects his interpretation of events in his environment. For example, although he has observed a clock's mechanism and has had its operation explained to him, it is unlikely that he will understand why a clock ticks or how it keeps time. Similarly, the reasons for the transformation of water to ice and back to water are not obvious. In addition to the child's restricted experience, there may be something about the very nature of his thought processes that differentiates his thinking from that of the adult. In other words, there probably are qualitative as well as quantitative differences between children and adults in their thinking and reasoning.

Piaget, the Swiss psychologist, has presented a theoretical framework describing stages in children's thinking based in part on his brilliant observations of his own three children. With respect to the child's explanation of physical events, Piaget argued that the child moves from a "precausal" reasoning stage, characterized by nonnaturalistic explanations based on magic, animism, and supernaturalism, to a rational or logical level in which naturalistic explanations of events are given. A number of factors account for this transition: mental maturity, increased ranged of experiences and familiarity with various natural phenomena, and the child's ability to separate himself from his world and to view events in objective rather than subjective terms.

PURPOSE

The present observation is designed to investigate age differences in children's concepts of physical causality.

SUBJECTS

Select approximately 5 children from each of two age groups: 5-6 years and 9-10 years.

PROCEDURE

Administer the following questionnaire to the children individually and record their responses. What makes:

1. a clock tick?
2. the wind blow?
3. airplanes crash?
4. a car move?
5. the clouds move?
6. ships sink?
7. a bicycle go?
8. it rain on some days?
9. a roof leak?
10. leaves fall from the trees in the fall?
11. the stars shine?
12. tires go flat?
13. balloons go up in the air?
14. rainbows come after the rain?
15. waves in the water?

16. the sun shine on some days but not on others?
17. a kite fly?
18. it get dark?
19. shadows?
20. the moon change shapes?
21. boats stay on top of the water?
22. it thunder?
23.
24. (Add several of your own choosing.)
25.

Classify the responses into the following two categories:

1. Nonnaturalistic – nonmaterialistic explanations involving spirits, magic or irrelevant or coincidental circumstances.

   For example: "Why do leaves fall of the trees in the fall?"

   "Because when winter's coming they can't stay on."

   "Why is it that we sometimes have rainbows after the rain?"

   "Because the sky makes it."

2. Naturalistic – explanations are logical or materialistic although not necessarily correct.

   For example: "Why do leaves fall off the trees in the fall?"

   "They turn different colors and fall off because they die."

   "Why is it that we sometimes have rainbows after the rain?"

   "The sun is red and the sky is blue and the clouds are white, so they all come together and you see all the colors together and that's a rainbow."

RESULTS

Compare the number of naturalistic versus nonnaturalistic explanations for the two age levels for each item separately. Put these data in tabular form as follows:

Item Number	*Nonnaturalistic*		*Naturalistic*	
	5-6 years	*9-10 years*	*5-6 years*	*9-10 years*

DISCUSSION

1. Do your results show clear age differences in type of explanation offered?
2. Did you find difficulty in classifying the responses? Explain.
3. Were there any marked differences among the items in type of explanation? What might account for these item differences?
4. Were you able to identify any factors that might account for the kind or level of explanation given by a child, such as intellectual level, breadth of experiences, personality characteristics, curiosity, or verbal ability?
5. What did you learn about children and their thinking from this observation?

SELECTED BIBLIOGRAPHY

Berzonsky, M. D. The role of familiarity in children's explanations of physical causality. *Child Development,* 1971, **42**, 705-715.

Deutsche, J. M. *The development of children's concepts of causal relations.* Minneapolis: University of Minnesota Press, 1937.

Huang, I. Children's conceptions of physical causality: A critical summary. *Journal of Genetic Psychology,* 1943, **63**, 71-121.

Inhelder, B., & Piaget, J. *The growth of logical thinking from childhood to adolescence.* New York: Basic Books, 1958.

Laurendeau, M., & Pinard, A. *Causal thinking in the child.* New York: International Universities Press, 1962.

Looft, W. Animistic thought in children: Understanding of "living" across its associated attributes. *Journal of Genetic Psychology,* 1974, **124**, 235-240.

Nass, M. L. The effects of three variables on children's concepts of physical causality. *Journal of Abnormal and Social Psychology,* 1956, **53**, 191-196.

Piaget, J. *The child's conception of physical causality.* London: Kegan Paul, 1930, (Republished: Totowa, N. J.: Littlefield, Adams, 1966).

Russell, D. H. *Children's thinking.* New York: Ginn, 1956.

Smeets, P. The animism controversy revisited: A probability analysis. *Journal of Genetic Psychology,* 1973, **123**, 219-225.

Observation 20

Labeling and Memory

The extremely important role played by language in intellectual development and in learning cannot be overemphasized. Words have been called "fishhooks in the mind." Having a label for an object or a concept facilitates the child's ability to deal with that object or concept—to understand it, to use it, and to remember it. Consequently, the larger a child's vocabulary, the better able he is to function intellectually. Language and intelligence are so closely related that is extremely difficult to assess them separately, although some nonverbal measures of intelligence have been developed. Even in these, however, it is likely that the child's verbal ability enables him to solve problems that require no verbal response from him. For example, in the problem on the next page, the child is asked to choose the figure on the right that would come next in the sequence on the left.

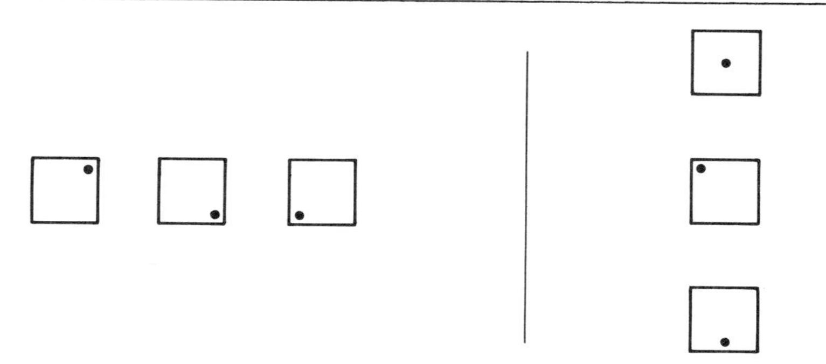

In the process of attempting to solve this problem, "spontaneous verbalization," though covert, might proceed something like this: "Let me see, first the dot is up there (upper right hand corner, if the child possesses these verbal labels); then it's down in that corner; next it's over in the other corner. I see, it's moving around like the hands on a clock, so next the dot would be up there. The right answer is the one over there in the middle." A child low in language usage would be markedly handicapped on such a problem.

A rich language environment in the early years enables the child to master the academic tasks required for school achievement. Children from homes where language is restricted and stereotyped and where it is used primarily to convey emotional expression ("Shut up, and do what your told."), rather than as a vehicle for thought, are handicapped in dealing with abstract ideas in the school learning situation.

PURPOSE

The purpose of this observation is to examine the role of language in memory.

SUBJECTS

Select two groups of five children each in the four to six year age range.

PROCEDURE

Assemble approximately a dozen common objects or pictures of objects, such as car, comb, shoe, chair, cap, house, spoon, book, watch (a great number of small plastic objects are available in variety stores). Show each child the objects one at a time for approximately 5 seconds. Hide the objects and ask the child to name as many as he can remember. The two groups will differ only in that the "Verbal-Label" group is asked to name each object as it is shown, while the other group is asked only to look at the objects. Record the objects recalled for each child.

RESULTS

Compare the "memory scores" for the two groups.

DISCUSSION

1. How do you explain the superior performance of the "Verbal-Label" group?
2. Do you have any evidence that the non-Verbal-Label group might have labeled the objects covertly?
3. What did you learn from this observation?

SELECTED BIBLIOGRAPHY

Blank, M., & Frank, S. Story recall in kindergarten children: Effect of method of presentation on psycholinguistic performance. *Child Development*, 1971, **42**, 299-312.

Bousfield, W. A. The occurrence of clustering in the recall of randomly arranged associates. *Journal of Genetic Psychology*, 1953, **49**, 229-240.

Brown, A., & Scott, M. Recognition memory for pictures in preschool children. *Journal of Experimental Child Psychology*, 1971, **11**, 401-412.

Cole, M., Frankel, F., & Sharp, D. Development of free recall learning in children. *Developmental Psychology*, 1971, **4**, 109-123.

Hagen, J., & Kingsley, P. Labeling effects in short-term memory. *Child Development*, 1968, **39**, 113-121.

Horowitz, L., Lampel, A., & Takanishi, R. The child's memory for unitized scenes. *Journal of Experimental Child Psychology*, 1969, **8**, 375-388.

Kobasigawa, A. Utilization of retrieval cues by children in recall. *Child Development*, 1974, **45**, 127-134.

Kossuth, G., Carroll, W., & Rogers, C. Free recall of words and objects. *Developmental Psychology*, 1971, **4**, 480.

Lange, G., & Hultsch, D. The development of free classification and

free recall in children. *Developmental Psychology*, 1970, **3**, 408.
Rossi, S., & Wittrock, M. Developmental shifts in verbal recall between mental ages two and five. *Child Development*, 1971, **42**, 333-338.
Schaeffer, B., Lewis, J., & Decar, A. The growth of children's semantic memory: Semantic elements. *Journal of Experimental Child Psychology*, 1971, **11**, 296-309.
Steinmetz, J., & Battig, W. Clustering and priority of free recall of newly learned items in children. *Developmental Psychology*, 1969, **1**, 503-507.
Tulving, E. Subjective organization in free recall of "unrelated" words. *Psychology Review*, 1962, **69**, 344-354.

Observation 21

Children's Play Preferences

Children's games and play activities have attracted the attention of psychologists, sociologists, anthropologists, and educators for a long time. Many definitions of play have been formulated. Some of these are as follows:

> Spencer: Activity performed for the immediate gratification derived, without regard for ulterior benefits; Lazarus: Play is activity which is in itself free, aimless, amusing or diverting; Seashore: *Free self expression* for the pleasure of expression; Dewey: Activities not consciously performed for the sake of any result beyond themselves; Stern: Play is voluntary, self-sufficient activity; Patrick: Those human activities which are free and spontaneous and which are pursued for their own sake alone, interest in them is self-sustaining, and they are not continued under any internal or external compulsion; Allin: Play refers to those activities which are accompanied by a state of comparative pleasure, exhilaration, power, and the feeling of self-initiative; Curti: Highly motivated activity which, as free from conflicts is usually, though not always, pleasurable.
>
> (Mitchell and Mason, 1934, 86-87)

A number of theories have been proposed to explain the functions served by play in the child's life. One of the earliest theories considered play as resulting from surplus energy. In order to release excess energy, children engage in play activities. Another point of view, sometimes called the relaxation theory of play, regards play as a way to replenish energy that has been drained off due to fatigue or anxiety. In a third theory, play is seen as a preexercise of developing instincts. For example, the little girl's interest in playing with dolls and in playing house in an early "exercise" of the maternal instinct. In a similar vein, some theorists have seen play as the child's way of obtaining practice in mastering skills that will be required later in adult life, and practicing them in an atmosphere free of stress and anxiety. Other theories regard play as an opportunity for the child to differentiate between reality and fantasy; as a phase through which a child passes in his attempts to learn about his environment; and as a way for the child to release and to "work through" or resolve some of his problems and anxieties.

The fact that animals engage in play suggests some biological functions served by such activities. Kittens, puppies, colts, monkeys, and porpoises are examples of species that have been observed in a variety of playful activities. Some of these clearly involve social interaction, while others involve an exploration of and interaction with the physical environment.

Cross-cultural studies of play suggest that the kinds of games engaged in by children in a given culture are related to certain aspects of that culture. An obvious example is that games of physical skill have been shown to occur in primitive cultures where there is spear-throwing and hunting. Further, whether the games predominating in a culture emphasize chance or strategy depends on some of the life conditions and values of that culture.

A number of aspects of play have been investigated. For example, changes with age in children's play preferences have been noted, with an increase with age in complexity and organization of games. A strong element of competition has been observed in the games of children beginning at about the age of eight years. Differences in play activities related to intelligence and such aspects of the environment as rural vs. urban setting have been studied. A recent interest in children's play has focused on sex differences in game choices in which preferences for certain kinds of play activities is used as a measure of masculinity and femininity in children. Several studies (Sutton-Smith, Rosenberg, & Morgan, 1963; Walker, 1964) have shown that with increasing age boys show an increased preference for such boy-type games as wrestling and football, while girls exhibit less clearcut sex typing in their game preferences as they get older. In fact, there are some masculine-type games for which girls show increased preference with age. Thus, although there are clear sex differences in game preferences at sixth grade, they are less marked than at the third grade level. With respect to sex differences in game performance, it appears that children perform best when they believe that a particular game is appropriate or suitable for their sex.

PURPOSE

The purpose of this observation is to examine children's play preferences over two age levels and the reasons given by children for their preferences.

METHOD

Subjects. Choose approximately three girls and three boys at the third and sixth grade levels.

Procedure. Administer individually the list of games found on pages 149 to 150. Ask the child to check those games that he likes to play best. If he experiences any difficulty in reading some of the words, provide assistance. Following the child's completion of the list, select five to ten of the games checked and ask him why he likes those games. Record his responses.

RESULTS

Compare the games by age level and by sex. Attempt to identify some patterns emerging from the reasons given by the children for their choices.

DISCUSSION

1. Did your results support the finding that there are greater sex differences at the third grade level than at the sixth grade?
2. Did the reasons given by the children confirm the notion that game choices are an index of masculinity-femininity? That is, was mention made of the sex-appropriateness of the games?
3. From the reasons given, can you conclude anything about the functions served in the child's life by engaging in play activities?
4. Did your results provide evidence for any of the theories put forth to explain play behavior in children?
5. What did you learn from this observation?

SELECTED BIBLIOGRAPHY

Avedon, E., & Sutton-Smith, B. *The study of games.* New York: Wiley, 1971.

Foster, J. C. Play activities of children in the first six grades. *Child Development*, 1930, **1**, 248-254.

Herron, R. E., & Sutton-Smith, B. *Child's play.* New York: Wiley, 1971.

Lehman, H. C., & Witty, P. A. *The psychology of play activities.* Barnes, 1927.

Mitchell, E. D., & Mason, B. S. *The theory of play.* New York: Barnes, 1948.

Montemayor, R. Children's performance in a game and their attraction to it as a function of sex-typed labels. *Child Development*, 1974, **45**, 152-156.

Rosenberg, B. G., & Sutton-Smith, B. A revised conception of masculine-feminine differences in play activities. *Journal of Genetic Psychology*, 1960, **96**, 165-170.

Sutton-Smith, B., Rosenberg, B. G., & Morgan, E. F., Jr. Development of sex differences in play choices during preadolescence. *Child Development*, 1963, **34**, 119-126.

Walker, R. N. Measuring masculinity and femininity by children's games choices. *Child Development*, 1964, **35**, 961-971.

Children's Games

_______ Bandits
_______ Baseball
_______ Basketball
_______ Bingo
_______ Blind Man's buff
_______ Boating
_______ Bows and errors
_______ Boxing
_______ Build forts or huts
_______ Build snowmen
_______ Camping
_______ Cartwheels
_______ Capture the flag
_______ Cars
_______ Chess
_______ Clay modeling
_______ Clue
_______ Climb trees
_______ Cooking
_______ Cops and robbers
_______ Cowboys
_______ Crack the whip
_______ Dancing
_______ Darts
_______ Dolls
_______ Doctors
_______ Dodgeball
_______ Dog and bone
_______ Draw or paint
_______ Dressing up
_______ Drop the handkerchief
_______ Farmer in the dell
_______ Fishing
_______ Follow the leader
_______ Football
_______ Fox and geese
_______ Gardening
_______ Giant steps
_______ Give plays
_______ Hide and seek
_______ Hide the thimble
_______ Hiking
_______ Hockey
_______ Hopscotch
_______ Horses
_______ House
_______ Huckle buckle beanstalk
_______ Hunting
_______ In and out the windows
_______ Indian wrestling
_______ I've got a secret
_______ Jacks

Children's Games continued

_______ Jump rope
_______ Jungle gym
_______ Kick ball
_______ King of the castle
_______ Knife
_______ Leap frog
_______ London bridge
_______ Make model planes
_______ Make scrapbooks
_______ Mulberry bush
_______ Musical chairs
_______ Name that tune
_______ Parchesi
_______ Pick up sticks
_______ Pillow fights
_______ Pitch horseshoes
_______ Play records
_______ Post office
_______ Push-up and sit-ups
_______ Puzzles
_______ Racing
_______ Read books
_______ Red light
_______ Red rover
_______ Ride horses
_______ Ring around the rosy
_______ Roller skate
_______ School
_______ Scrabble
_______ See-saw
_______ Sewing
_______ Shooting
_______ Shoot pool
_______ Simon says
_______ Sledding
_______ Soccer
_______ Soldiers
_______ Spacemen
_______ Spin the bottle
_______ Spin tops
_______ Statues
_______ Stoop tag
_______ Store
_______ Swings
_______ Tag
_______ Tail on the donkey
_______ Throw snowballs
_______ Tic tac toe
_______ Tiddley winks
_______ Toy trains
_______ Use tools
_______ Volley ball
_______ Weight lifting
_______ Work with machines
_______ Wrestling

Observation 22

Reflection-Impulsivity in Children

A great many childhood personality traits or dimensions have been examined. These have included dependence-independence, aggression, anxiety, conscience, dominance-submissiveness, altruism, and social acceptance or sociability. Various factors, such as the child's relationship with his parents, have been explored in an attempt to understand the way in which these personality characteristics develop and the ways in which they are affected by and modified by experiences in the early years. Clearly, the parents' attitudes toward the child and toward childrearing influence the development of dependency and aggressiveness, for example. Increasing recognition is given to the fact that parents serve as models for the child; he tends to copy or imitate their behavior. A parent who is kind, considerate, and thoughtful in his relations with others is likely to have children who manifest similar behaviors. Likewise, children with a highly developed conscience and a strong sense of responsibility are probably reflecting similar characteristics in their parents.

The role played by genetic and physiological factors in the development of certain personality characteristics is not clearly understood. For example, there is some evidence for a genetic basis for the dominance-submission and the extraversion-introversion dimensions. Needless to say, an adult's personality and behavior are the result of a continual interplay between heredity and environment, between genetic and experiential factors.

The reflection-impulsivity dimension in children has received considerable attention in recent research. When faced with various problem solving tasks, some children approach the task with great caution and deliberation. They reach a decision or a solution only after carefully weighing alternate solutions. Impulsive children, on the other hand, spend little time in considering alternatives. They make quick and hasty judgments that frequently result in incorrect responses.

Kagan (1965) has called the reflection-impulsivity dimension a measure of the child's "conceptual tempo." Research has demonstrated that differences in this dimension appear early, even in infancy; that it is stable over time; that decision time (reflection) increases from grades one through four; and that this dimension is related to such other variables as reading errors and inductive reasoning. In general, as compared with impulsive children, reflective ones have been found to have a longer attention span, and are less distractible and less active motor-wise. Taken together, these findings suggest that the reflection-impulsivity dimension may well play an important role in the child's school success. Moreover, assuming that this personality variable is modifiable (even though there may be a physiological basis for it), training programs could be developed so that highly impulsive children may be shown a more effective strategy in approaching learning tasks. Indeed, a study of impulsive second grade children (Egeland, 1974) found that training improved their performance on the Matching Familiar Figures Test described below; moreover, this improvement generalized to the child's performance on a measure of reading achievement.

To assess reflection-impulsivity, a Matching Familiar Figures test (MFF) was developed by Kagan and coworkers (Kagan, Rosman, Day, Albert, & Phillips, 1964). This test consists of a series of twelve pictures, each on a separate sheet, along with six variants of that picture. The child is asked to select the picture that is exactly like the one at the top of the sheet. The two measures obtained from this procedure are response time (the amount of time the child takes to make his choice) and the number of errors. Since recent research (Block, Block, & Harrington, 1974) suggests that accuracy is a more important variable than latency (response time) the student should be particularly alerted to fast/inaccurate responses.

PURPOSE

This observational study is designed to explore the assessment of reflection-impulsivity in children and to investigate the relation between this dimension and several aspects of motor behavior.

METHOD

Subjects. Select approximately ten children from grade 1-3.

Procedure. Test each child individually using the picture materials on pages 155–162. Ask the child to find the picture that is exactly like the one at the top of the page. Record the number of errors made and the response time (in seconds) for each picture–that is, the length of time the child takes to make his selection.

Two tasks involving fine motor control will be used to assess motor behavior. On page 161 ask the child to connect the dots in order to make umbrellas. Give the following instructions: "The game here is to connect the four dots in each square in order to make umbrellas. The handles have already been drawn in. Someone has connected the four dots in the first square up here to show us how to do it. See, there is a straight line across here and a curved line up here. Your job is to see how fast you can draw lines connecting the four dots in every square to make 16 umbrellas. But be careful. Be sure to hit all four dots. Go ahead."

For the second task, use the worksheet on page 162. Give the following instructions: "Now on this page I want to see how *fast* you can draw a path for the dog to run from here (point to the dog) over to get his bone here (point to the bone). A broken line has been drawn to show where the path is but your job is to connect the lines so the dog can run along the path. See how fast you can draw the path but be sure to connect all the broken lines."

Record the amount of time taken to complete each task. In addition, make a general or global assessment of the child's performance in terms of some of the following criteria: (1) accuracy of performance; (2) did the child appear to map out a plan of action before beginning or did he proceed immediately with the task? (3) did the child exhibit good motor control or was he somewhat poorly coordinated in performing the tasks? (4) To what extent did the child appear tense and anxious?

RESULTS

Compare the children's performance on the two sets of tasks.

DISCUSSION

1. Was there agreement between the results of the MFF test and the children's performance on the motor control tasks?
2. How well do you think the MFF test really measures the reflection-impulsivity variable? In other words, did you find any other evidence to support the fact that children with short response times on the MFF test behave impulsively in other situations?
3. If the children who appeared impulsive on the MFF test showed somewhat poor and erratic motor control, might this indicate a physiological basis for impulsivity?
4. What might be included in a training program to modify the behavior of impulsive children, assuming that reflective behavior is desirable?
5. What did you learn from this observation about the reflection-impulsivity dimension and about children?

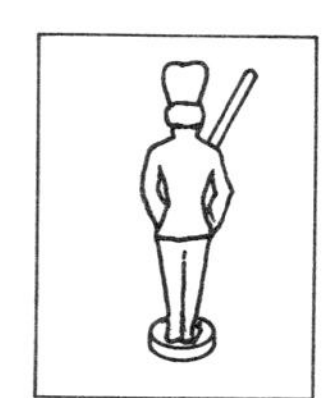

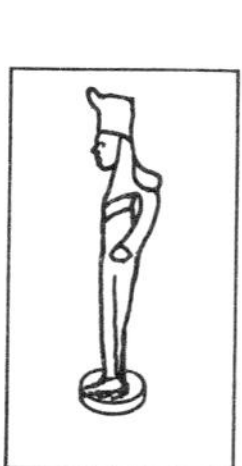

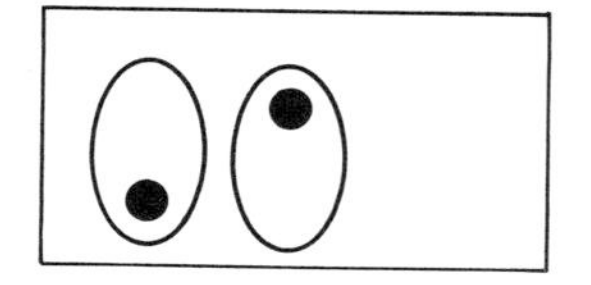

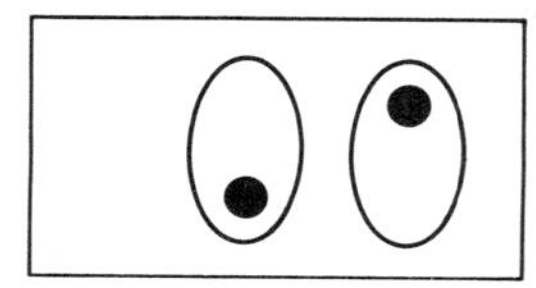

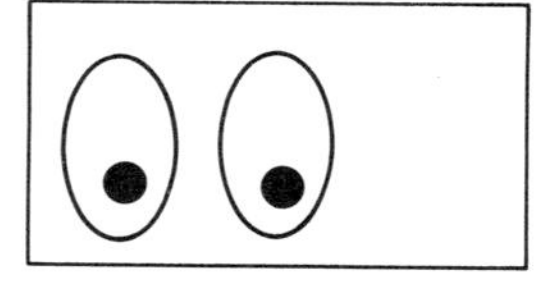

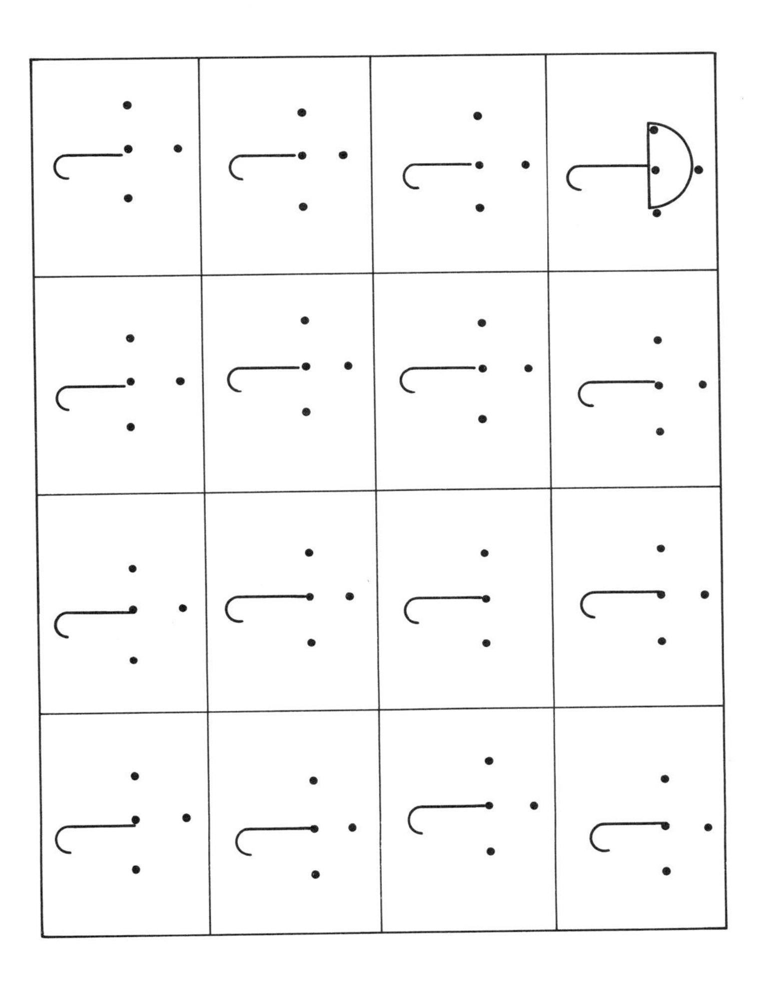

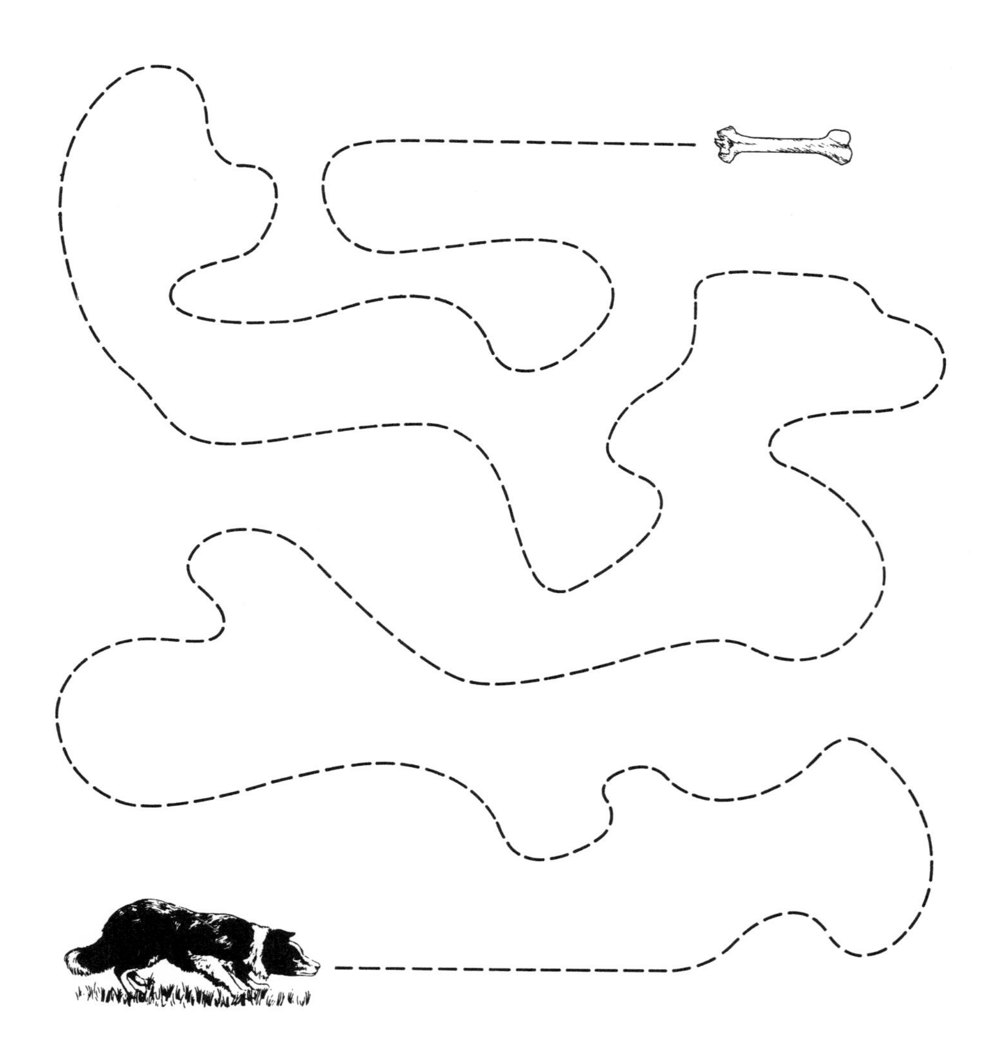

SELECTED BIBLIOGRAPHY

Ault, R. Problem-solving strategies of reflective, impulsive, fast-accurate, and slow-inaccurate children. *Child Development*, 1973, **44**, 259-266.

Bjorklund, D., & Butter, E. Can cognitive impulsivity be predicted from classroom behavior? *Journal of Genetic Psychology*, 1973, **123**, 185-194.

Block, J., Block, J. H., & Harrington, D. Some misgivings about the Matching Familiar Figures Test as a measure of reflection-impulsivity. *Developmental Psychology*, 1974, **10**, 611-632.

Egeland, B. Training impulsive children in the use of more efficient scanning techniques. *Child Development*, 1974, **45**, 165-171.

Eska, B., & Black, K. Conceptual tempo in young grade-school children. *Child Development*, 1971, **42**, 505-516.

Kagan, J. Reflection-impulsivity and reading ability in primary grade children. *Child Development*, 1965, **36**, 609-628.

Kagan, J. Reflection-impulsivity: The generality and dynamics of conceptual tempo. *Journal of Abnormal Psychology*, 1966, **71**, 17-24.

Kagan, J., Pearson, L., & Welch, L. The modifiability of an impulsive tempo. *Journal of Educational Psychology*, 1966, **57**, 359-365.

Kagan, J., Rosman, B., Day, D., Albert, J., & Phillips, W. Information processing in the child: significance of analytic and reflective attitudes. *Psychological Monographs*, 1964, **78**, (1, Whole No. 578).

Katz, J. Reflection-impulsivity and color-form sorting. *Child Development*, 1971, **42**, 745-754.

Mann, L. Differences between reflective and impulsive children in tempo and quality of decision making. *Child Development*, 1973, **44**, 274-279.

Meichenbaum, D., & Goodman, J. Reflection-impulsivity and verbal control of motor behavior. *Child Development*, 1969, **40**, 785-797.

Messer, S., Kagan, J., & McCall, R. Fixation time and tempo of play in infants. *Developmental Psychology*, 1970, **3**, 406.

Reali, N., & Hall, V. Effect of success and failure on the reflective and impulsive child. *Developmental Psychology*, 1970, **3**, 392-402.

Siegelman, E. Reflective and impulsive observing behavior. *Child Development*, 1969, **40**, 1213-1222.

Ward, W. Reflection-impulsivity in kindergarten children. *Child Development*, 1968, **39**, 867-874.

Observation 23

Locus of Control

Perhaps one of the most important aspects of motivation is the individual's belief that, in some measure, he is in control of his own destiny, that his actions do determine the outcome of his life experiences. Certainly people at all age levels differ markedly in the extent to which they believe they are at the mercy of external forces versus the extent to which they are responsible for events that occur in their lives. This psychological variable has been called "external versus internal locus of control."

Scales tapping this dimension were developed first for adults (Rotter, 1966). More recently, several scales have been constructed for children (Crandall, Katkovsky, & Crandall, 1965; Nowicki & Strickland, 1971). The research using these scales has revealed a number of interesting relationships. First, there are changes with age in this dimension, with older children showing greater internal locus of control than younger children. Some social class differences exist, with children from lower social class backgrounds and from minority groups exhibiting an external orientation. Indeed, this may represent a realistic appraisal of their social condition in which their families have little power to influence those events that affect their lives.

The child's school achievement has been found to be related to the locus of control dimension. This is reasonable since the child's motivation to achieve and his achievement behavior are a reflection of the fact that he believes that his school grades are determined, not by chance or by the teacher's whims, but by his own efforts.

As compared with later-born children, first-borns are more internally oriented. Typically first-borns are required to assume more responsibility in the family, and thus they develop a strong sense of inner responsibility. Younger children, on the other hand, are often led to believe that they will be taken care of by others.

While few sex differences in locus of control have been found, there does appear to be a stronger relation for boys than for girls between locus of control orientation and school achievement. That is, boys who possess a strong internal locus of control are more likely than girls to show high school achievement. This suggests that in our society, belief that one is responsible for one's own successes is a stronger motivation for academic achievement striving in males than in females.

Some important relationships have been found between several parental behaviors and attitudes and the child's ability to accept personal responsibility for what happens to him. Boys whose parents are positive, warm, and approving toward them are more likely to accept such responsibility. Parental acceptance provides the boy with the kind of security that permits him to assume responsibility for his successes and for his failures. A similar relationship, but less pronounced, exists for girls.

Sociologists (e.g., Riesman, 1953) have argued that our society is becoming increasingly characterized by an "outer-directed" rather than an "inner-directed" orientation. People feel powerless and alienated in a vast and complex society. The individual believes he has few avenues through which he can exert some influence on political and governmental forces. Consequently, he retreats from active participation in national as well as community affairs. Individual achievement and effort, once the ultimate value in our society, is replaced by a feeling of helplessness and a refusal to accept personal responsibility for one's own actions and destiny.

PURPOSE

This observation is designed to explore in some depth differences among children in the locus of control dimension.

METHOD

Subjects. Select five to six children in the fourth through sixth grades. Should the student be particularly interested in motivation for school achievement, he might select a group of children designated by the teacher as underachievers.

Procedure. Administer to the subjects the Nowicki-Strickland Personal Reaction Survey found on page 170-171.

Based on an examination of the Survey and your own ideas regarding locus of control, construct a brief interview schedule designed to tap the children's reasons for believing the way they do. For example, you might ask, "Why is it some kids always seem to get the worst end of things in school? Is it their fault? Or do others just have it in for them? Is there anything they can do about it? Or is it just their bad luck?" Do not be rigid in following your list of questions. Try to follow the child's thinking and probe further without disrupting his train of thought and without suggesting answers to him. Interview the children individually and record their responses. Based on the interview, attempt to rate each child on the following continuum:

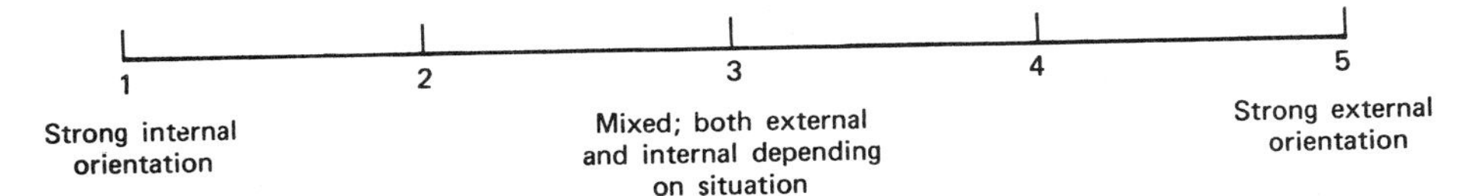

RESULTS

Examine the relation between the children's responses on the locus of control scale and their responses to the interview questions. Attempt to identify some patterns (in their reasoning) regarding their beliefs and attitudes expressed in the interviews.

DISCUSSION

1. Based on your comparisons of the children's responses to the interview and to the survey, do you feel that the latter adequately assesses locus of control? What kinds of questions would you include in such a scale?
2. What kinds of information emerged from the interviews? Were your questions useful in getting at the locus of control dimension?
3. Based on the interview responses, could you speculate concerning the reasons why children develop the orientation they do with respect to accepting personal responsibility for what happens to them?
4. What might be some of the kinds of topics you would include in a program designed to modify a child's external orientation? Indeed, do you think it would be desirable to attempt such a modification program?
5. What did you learn from this observation?

SELECTED BIBLIOGRAPHY

Cohen, S., & Oden, S. An examination of creativity and locus of control in children. *Journal of Genetic Psychology*, 1974, **124**, 179-185.

Crandall, V. C., Katkovsky, W., & Crandall, V. J. Children's belief in their own control of reinforcements in intellectual-academic achievement situations. *Child Development*, 1965, **36**, 91-109.

Crandall, V. J., Katkovsky, W., & Preston, A. Motivational and ability determinants of young children's intellectual achievement behaviors. *Child Development*, 1962, **33**, 643-661.

Gruen, G., Korte, J., & Baum, J. Group measure of locus of control. *Developmental Psychology*, 1974, **10**, 683-686.

Katkovsky, W., Crandall, V. C., & Good, S. Parental antecedents of children's beliefs in internal-external control of reinforcements in intellectual achievement situations. *Child Development*, 1967, **38**, 765-776.

Lifshitz, M. Internal-external locus-of-control dimension as a function of age and the socialization milieu. *Child Development*, 1973, **44**, 538-546.

McGhee, P. E., & Crandall, V. C. Beliefs in internal-external control of reinforcements and academic performance. *Child Development*, 1968, **39**, 91-102.

Nowicki, S., & Segal, W. Perceived parental characteristics, locus of control orientation, and behavioral correlates of locus of control. *Developmental Psychology*, 1974, **10**, 33-37.

Nowicki, S., & Strickland, B. A locus of control scale for children. Paper presented at American Psychological Association meetings, Washington, D. C., 1971.

Nowicki, S., & Walker, C. Achievement in relation to locus of control: Identification of a new source of variance. *Journal of Genetic Psychology*, 1973, **123**, 63-67.

Riesman, D. (with N. Glazer & R. Denny). *The lonely crowd: A study of the changing American character.* New Haven: Yale University Press, 1953.

Rotter, J. B. Generalized expectancies for internal versus external control of reinforcement. *Psychological Monographs*, 1966, **80**, 1-28.

The N-S Personal Reaction Survey

Yes	No		
_______	_______	1.	Are some kids just born lucky?
_______	_______	2.	Do you feel that most of the time it doesn't pay to try hard because things never turn out right anyway?
_______	_______	3.	Do you feel that most of the time parents listen to what their children have to say?
_______	_______	4.	Do you believe that wishing can make good things happen?
_______	_______	5.	Do you feel that it's nearly impossible to change your parent's mind about anything?
_______	_______	6.	Do you feel that when you do something wrong there's very little you can do to make it right?
_______	_______	7.	Do you believe that most kids are just born good at sports?
_______	_______	8.	Are most of the other kids your age stronger than you are?
_______	_______	9.	Do you feel that one of the best ways to handle most problems is just not to think about them?
_______	_______	10.	If you find a four leaf clover do you believe that it might bring you good luck?
_______	_______	11.	Do you feel that when a kid your age decides to hit you, there's little you can do to stop him or her?
_______	_______	12.	Have you felt that when people were mean to you it was usually for no reason at all?
_______	_______	13.	Do you believe that when bad things are going to happen they just are going to happen no matter what you try to do to stop them?

______ ______ 14. Most of the time do you find it useless to try to get your own way at home?

______ ______ 15. Do you feel that when somebody your age wants to be your enemy there's little you can do to change matters?

______ ______ 16. Do you usually feel that you have little to say about what you get to eat at home?

______ ______ 17. Do you feel that when someone doesn't like you there's little you can do about it?

______ ______ 18. Do you usually feel that it's almost useless to try in school because most other children are just plain smarter than you are?

______ ______ 19. Are you the kind of person who believes that planning ahead makes things turn out better?

______ ______ 20. Most of the time, do you feel that you have little to say about what your family decides to do?

Observation 24

Social Interaction Among Preschoolers

Social groups wield a tremendously powerful influence on their members. This is true whether the group is a somewhat formally structured and organized one such as a Boy Scout troop or a rather loosely knit neighborhood group of children. The perception of an individual by his peers (e.g., his fellow third-graders, office workers, society club members, inmates) is insightful and, at times, harsh. Sociologists have argued that the way we see ourselves is, in large part, a reflection of how others see us. The nature of our interaction with others affects us primarily because such interactions are repetitive. Patterns become established that are quite constant and stable over long periods of time. For example, one study (Bonney, 1943) found that a child's social position in the peer group from grades one through five was as constant as his intellectual and academic achievement. Moreover, friendships have been found to become increasingly stable throughout childhood and adolescence. One reason for the stability of popularity and social acceptance over time is that children of greatly differing ages agree on the kinds of qualities they like and dislike in others. These include a long list of characteristics: social class background, school achievement, cooperativeness, responsibility, good health, empathy, attractiveness of appearance, cheerfulness, fairness, sex-appropriate behavior, kindness, trustworthiness, honesty, sense of humor, sincerity, and active participation in various activities. Children who are aggressive, unfriendly, attention-seeking, and dependent on adults frequently are not liked by peers.

While a great many studies have been devoted to identifying differences among children in the quality and the quantity of their social interactions, amazingly few have attempted to discover reasons for these differences. Why, for example, do some four-year-olds interact harmoniously with peers in a nursery school setting while the interaction of others is marked by conflict and rejection? The fact that such differences appear so early suggests the importance of the child's early relationships within the family setting. One might speculate concerning the importance of parental acceptance of the child and the security that this gives him—the security which permits him to interact with others in mutually satisfying ways.

Two other aspects of social interaction have received relatively little attention. First, is it possible to modify or improve the level of a child's acceptance by agemates? Can a child be shown better ways of interacting with others, and will such an approach affect his behavior? The answer to these questions may depend in part on the reasons for the child's poor social relations. Social rejection may reflect deep personality maladjustment, or, somewhat more simply, it may indicate that the child has not learned techniques or strategies that result in positive responses from others. A series of studies by Hartup, Charlesworth, and co-workers has shown that acceptance by peers is related to the frequency with which a child gives positive reinforcement (approval, affection, praise, offers help, and gives objects such as toys) to peers.

A second aspect of social interaction about which we know relatively little concerns the long range consequences of childhood social relations. Can we predict an individual's adult behavior and adjustment from the kinds of social interactions he experienced in his growing up years? Roff (1961) has shown that the adequacy of an adult's adjustment to military service can be predicted from his early peer relations. Specifically, men who received bad conduct discharges from military service frequently had a history of early peer rejection. However, whether a similar relationship holds between good childhood social relations and adult adjustment remains to be shown. Perhaps sociability, as we define it in childhood and adolescence, is less important in the adult years where one's close social contacts become somewhat restricted and where other aspects of life (job satisfaction, solitary interests, and family relations) assume greater importance.

PURPOSE

The purpose of this study is to observe the frequency of social interaction among preschoolers and the general positiveness or negativeness of this interaction.

METHOD

Subjects. Observe a preschool (three- to five-year-olds) group in a nursery school situation.

Procedure. Before beginning the observation, familiarize yourself with the children and with the nursery school setting. It is important that the children accept your presence as an observer. Choose a general free play activity period for observation when there is a minimum of adult structuring of the situation.

Observe each child in turn for 3 minutes. Follow the alphabetical list of names so that your decision concerning which child to observe is not influenced by the occurrence of social interaction at that time. Place a check under the appropriate column for each social contact. In addition, indicate which child the subject under observation is interacting with by using the number assigned each child (or the child's name).

Observe on three different days so that each child is observed for a total of nine minutes. The separate days of observation will permit an estimate of the consistency of children's social behavior from one day to the next and will help to guard against the possibility that certain factors were present on a single day that altered or distorted the typical social interactions of the children. For example, the number of children as well as which particular children are present on a given day may affect the kinds of social interaction which occur.

The following behaviors will serve to define the two main interaction categories:

Positive social interaction: attending, offering praise and approval, offering help, smiling and laughing, verbal help, general conversation, physical and verbal affection, sharing, cooperating, giving physical objects such as toys or food. *Negative social interaction:* noncompliance (refusing to cooperate, ignoring overtures from another), interference (taking property, disrupting or interfering with ongoing activity), derogation (ridicule, disapproval, blaming, tattling), and attack (physical attacks, threats).

Below is an example of the kind of recording sheet you might use for recording your observations.

Observation Schedule

General activity ____________ Date ____________

Number of children present ________ Time ____________

Children's Names	*Categories*	
	Positive social contact	*Negative social contact*
Anderson, Jean		
Baker, Tommy		
Cardona, Juan		
Denton, Lisa		

RESULTS

Tabulate the total number of social contacts for each child as well as the number of positive and negative interactions.

In addition, tabulate the number of different children with whom each child interacted.

Sum across children to get the total number of positive and negative contacts for the group as a whole. Also, sum these figures separately for the boys and girls.

Tabulate the above figures for each of the three days separately.

DISCUSSION

1. Did your findings agree with previous research that has found a higher proportion of positive than negative interactions at the preschool level?
2. Did you find a sex difference? Again, previous research has shown that boys experience a greater number of social contacts than girls.
3. In general did you find that preschoolers participate in more or fewer social interactions than you had expected?
4. Were there wide differences in your data among the three days? If so, what might have accounted for these differences?
5. What did you learn from this observation?

SELECTED BIBLIOGRAPHY

Biehler, R. Companion choice behavior in the kindergarten. *Child Development*, 1954, **25**, 45-50.

Challman, R. C. Factors influencing friendships among preschool children. *Child Development*, 1932, **3**, 146-158.

Charlesworth, R., & Hartup, W. W. Positive social reinforcement in the nursery school peer group. *Child Development*, 1967, **38**, 993-1002.

Deutsch, F. Observational and sociometric measures of peer popularity and their relationship to egocentric communication in female preschoolers. *Developmental Psychology*, 1974, **10**, 745-747.

Green, E. H. Friendships and quarrels among pre-school children. *Child Development*, 1959, **30**, 91-107.

Hartup, W. W., Glazer, & Charlesworth, R. Peer reinforcement and sociometric status. *Child Development*, 1967, **38**, 1017-1024.

Haskett, G. Modification of peer preferences of first-grade children. *Developmental Psychology*, 1971, **4**, 429-433.

Koch, H. L. Popularity in preschool children: Some related factors and a technique for its measurement. *Child Development*, 1933, **4**, 164-175.

Lippitt, R. Popularity among preschool children. *Child Development*, 1941, **12**, 305-322.

Marshall, H. R., & McCandless, B. A study in prediction of social behavior of preschool children. *Child Development*, 1957, **28**, 149-159.

McCandless, B., Bilous, C. B., & Bennett, H. L. Peer popularity and dependence on adults in preschool-age socialization. *Child Development*, 1961, **32**, 511-518.

Moore, S., & Updegraff, R. Sociometric status of preschool children related to age, sex, nurturance-giving, and dependency. *Child Development*, 1964, **35**, 519-524.

Parten M. Social participation among preschool children by a time sample technique. *Journal of Abnormal and Social Psychology*, 1932, **27**, 243-269.

Roff, M. Childhood social interactions and young adult bad conduct. *Journal of Abnormal and Social Psychology*, 1961, **63**, 333-337.

Schroeer, R., & Flapan, D. Assessing aggressive and friendly behaviors in young children. *Journal of Psychology*, 1971, **77**, 193-202.

Walters, J., Pearce, D., & Dahms, L. Affectional and aggressive behavior of preschool children. *Child Development*, 1957, **28**, 15-26.

Observation 25

Teacher-Pupil Interaction

Much of the early writing and research concerning the child's personality development dealt with his relationship with his parents. While no one would argue that the parents do not play a major initial role in laying the foundation for various behavioral patterns and attitudes, increasing recognition is being given to the importance of other aspects of the psychological environment, both within and outside of the family setting. The child's position in the family constellation and his ongoing relations with his siblings affect his personality development. Futhermore, as he gets older and moves outside the family, his social interaction with peers wields great influence. Also, adults other than the parents assume increasing importance.

With the beginning of school the child's world expands and becomes more complex. The sheer number of potential interactions increases greatly. For the next twelve to thirteen years the school and the social interactions that take place within the school setting are extremely important in shaping the child's view of himself and of the world: his feelings of acceptance or rejection by agemates; his feelings of adequacy and competency; his adoption of attitudes and values concerning human behavior.

The importance of the teacher in establishing the psychological atmosphere of the classroom cannot be overemphasized. A number of personal accounts have been written illustrating the tremendous, long lasting influence teachers have exerted on their pupils. The teacher may provide great support and encouragement or she may exhibit negative behaviors towards her pupils.

A number of observational studies of teacher-pupil interaction have been conducted using a variety of categories. These have included approval vs. disapproval, learner-centered vs. teacher-centered behavior, and dominative vs. integrative behavior. Social class background, sex of child, level of school achievement, and personality adjustment are variables that have been found to be related to the quantity and the quality of the child's interaction with his teacher. Teachers have been shown to have more favorable contacts with children of high economic status than with those from lower economic backgrounds. Boys receive more teacher disapproval than girls. Classroom observation has shown also that while low achievers experience more contact with the teacher, the teacher-pupil interaction of high achievers is more favorable.

While little research is available on the effects of various teacher-pupil interactions on the child's adjustment, certain kinds of psychological relations between teacher and children are certainly far more conducive than others to the emotional and intellectual well-being of children in a school setting. Human interaction is repetitive in nature and patterns become established. Thus, while a single incident of teacher disapproval may not affect a child, a pattern of such interaction over an extended period of time will result inevitably in certain unfavorable attitudes on the part of the child, unfavorable attitudes towards himself and towards school.

PURPOSE

This observational study is designed to investigate the distribution of teacher approval and disapproval among the pupils in a classroom.

METHOD

Subjects. Select an elementary school classroom grade 1-6.

Procedure. While most observational studies of teacher-pupil interaction in the classroom have employed a modified time sampling procedure using time intervals from 5 to 30 seconds, the present observation will note only the occurrence of a given behavior without breaking up the observation period into time units.

For observation, choose a time when academic instruction is in progress, either with the entire class or with a small group. Record the duration of your observation so determination can be made of the frequency of the teacher's behavior in the approval and disapproval categories.

$$\frac{\text{Number of teacher responses}}{\text{time}}$$

While the student may formulate his own definitions of approval and disapproval, the following definitions may be used. They include both verbal and nonverbal behavior.

> *Approval:* Makes positive valuation of some aspect of the child's performance with verbal praise ("You did a very nice job.") and non-verbal responses, such as smiling, nodding, making physical contact by patting, touching, or dispensing token or material rewards.
> *Disapproval:* Makes negative valuation of some aspect of child's performance through verbal criticism, correcting, reminding, admonishing, reproving, or expressing generally negative feelings ("You'd better get busy." "This is not your best work." "Stop fooling around.") and non-verbal valuation such as frowning, head shaking, or physical punishments.
>
> (Adapted from Goodwin & Meyerson, 1971)

Since, as mentioned above, research has shown that boys receive more teacher disapproval and girls more teacher approval, record sex of child to whom teacher is directing her response. Also, in order to identify the number of contacts received by each child, identify the children in some way. Learning their names is not necessary; perhaps numbers can be assigned on a seating chart.

RESULTS

1. What percent of the teacher's responses fell into the approval and disapproval categories? Use the following formula for percentage:

$$\frac{\text{Number of teacher approval responses}}{\text{Number of teacher approval + number of teacher disapproval}} \times 100$$

2. Did the teacher make more total responses to boys or to girls. Also, was there a sex difference in the approval vs. disapproval categories?
3. How evenly were the teacher's responses distributed among the members of the class? Did some students receive more responses than others? Did certain students receive primarily approval responses while other received disapproval responses?

DISCUSSION

1. Based on your observations, could you list some of the child behaviors that produced and/or preceded the teacher's behavior? In other words, for what kinds of child behavior did the teacher give approval and disapproval? How might this reflect the teacher's philosophy of teaching and how she views her role as a teacher?
2. What effects did the teacher's responses have on the children's behavior? How did the children react after receiving approval or disapproval?
3. Would you say that the classroom atmosphere established by the teacher was a positive, encouraging one or somewhat negative and restrictive in nature?
4. To what extent do you feel your relatively brief observation was an adequate sampling of the teacher's typical behavior?

SELECTED BIBLIOGRAPHY

Anderson, H. H. The measurement of domination and of socially integrative behavior in teachers' contacts with children. *Child Development*, 1939, **10**, 73-89.

Anderson, H. H. Domination and social integration in the behavior of kindergarten children and teachers. *Genetic Psychology Monographs*, 1939, **21**, 287-385.

Becker, W. C., Madsen, C. H., Arnold, C. R., & Thomas, D. R. The contingent use of teacher attention and praise in reducing classroom behavior problems. *Journal of Special Education*, 1967, **1**, 287-307.

DeGroat, A. F., & Thompson, G. G. A study of the distribution of teacher approval and disapproval among sixth-grade children. *Journal of Experimental Education*, 1949, **18**, 57-75.

Flanders, N. A., & Havumaki, S. The effect of teacher-pupil contacts involving praise on the sociometric choices of students. *Journal of Educational Psychology*, 1960, **51**, 65-68.

Goodwin, D. L., & Meyerson, D. Teacher-pupil interaction scale (TPIS). Unpublished manuscript, San Jose State College, 1971.

Harvey, O. J., Prather, M., White, B. J., Hoffmeister, J. Teachers' beliefs, classroom atmosphere and student behavior. *American Educational Research Journal*, 1968, **5**, 151-166.

Hoehn, A. H. A study of social class differentiation in the classroom behavior of nineteen third-grade teachers. *Journal of Social Psychology*, 1954, **39**, 269-292.

Medley, D., & Mitzel, H. A technique for measuring classroom behavior. *Journal of Educational Psychology*, 1958, **49**, 86-92.

Medley, D., & Mitzel, H. Measuring classroom behavior by systematic observation. In Gage, N. L. (Ed.) *Handbook of research on teaching*. Chicago; Rand McNally, 1963.

Meyer, W. J., & Thompson, G. G. Sex differences in the distribution of teacher approval and disapproval among sixth-grade children. *Journal of Educational Psychology*, 1956, **47**, 385-396.

Werry, J., & Quay, H. Observing the classroom behavior of elementary school children. *Exceptional Children*, 1969, **35**, 461-470.

Withall, J. The development of a technique for the measurement of social-emotional climates in classrooms. *Journal of Experimental Education*, 1949, **17**, 347-361.

Withall, J. Assessment of the social-emotional climates experienced by a group of seventh graders as they moved from class to class. *Educational and Psychological Measurement*, 1952, **12**, 440-451.